THE POWER OF BIBLICAL THINKING

Helping Hurting People by Using Powerful Principles and Insights From the Bible

By Ken Wilson, Ph.D.

Catalog Number C-3067

ISBN 1-56794-261-X

Copyright © 2002 Ken Wilson, Ph.D.

All rights reserved. No portion of this book may be reproduced in any form without the written permission of the publisher, including translation.

Published by
Star Bible Publications
P.O. Box 821220
Fort Worth, Texas 76182
800-433-7507

TABLE OF CONTENTS

Chapter		Page
1.	THE POWER OF THE MIND	7
2.	THE POWER OF SELF-TALK	19
3.	THE POWER OF SELF-CONTROL	31
4.	DEALING WITH ANGER ISSUES	45
5.	CREATING A POSITIVE SELF-WORTH	55
6.	CREATING POSITIVE COMMUNICATION	67
7.	BASIC PRINCIPLES OF CRISIS INTERVENTION	79
8.	THE AUTHORITY AND RELIABILITY OF SCRIPTURE	95
9.	THE DESIGN AND ORDER OF GOD'S CREATION	105
10.	REVIEW OF POPULAR COUNSELING THEORIES	115
11.	THE BIBLE AND CHRISTIAN ETHICS	127
12.	THE WORK OF THE HOLY SPIRIT	139
13.	THE TRUTH ABOUT SUFFERING	151
14.	CREATED IN GOD'S IMAGE	157
	SELECTED BIBLIOGRAPHY	171

A portion of chapter fourteen is adapted from the book "Temperament Therapy" by Richard Arno, Ph.D., used by permission of the National Christian Counselors Association, all rights reserved.

Examples cited in this book are composites of the author's actual cases in his work as a professional counselor. Names and facts have been changed and rearranged to maintain confidentiality.

All Scripture quotations, unless otherwise noted, are taken from the New International Version © 1986 by Holman Bible Publishers, all rights reserved.

ACKNOWLEDGEMENTS

When endeavoring to write a book, it is almost always a team effort. It is no different when it comes to the production of this book. I am surely indebted to my wife, Sandy, for helping edit the material and format. She has continued to be an encouragement to me in all my endeavors and I appreciate her very much.

Acknowledgements would not be complete without mentioning our church secretaries, Linda Chaffee, Darlene Childers, and Machelle Turner. Their continued support, as well as their editing and printing efforts, made this publication possible. They at times worked extra hours on the script believing that the results would be worth the effort and would help many people who would read this book. I appreciate and thank them for their efforts.

I also want to show my appreciation to the Sunset International Bible Institute and Virgil Yocham, Dean of External Studies, for their encouragement in writing this book and for their developing a Basic Counseling Course from this book.

Many of the thoughts and ideas in this book have been collected over an extended period of time. Some of this information comes from other sources originally, but I don't remember what they were. I am indebted to them, whomever and whatever, because they have contributed to my learning and this book.

And finally, I want to thank my good friend and colleague, Mike Allen. He was the inspiration for this book and the major contributor to the chapter on "The Basic Principles of Crisis Intervention." He conferred with me on many issues and because he is a professional counselor, as well as a minister, I appreciate his input greatly.

Our goal has been to provide a book with material for the Christian leader and believer, who wishes to be an effective Skilled Helper in reaching out to those who are in crisis and despair with the healing truth of God's Word. I hope and pray that this book will help in some way to accomplish that goal.

Ken Wilson, Ph.D.
Tacoma, Washington

INTRODUCTION

Many people have problems in our world today. Some don't get along with their spouses, some are full of anxiety over their job security, some have troubling worries about their indebtedness and many are depressed and empty inside.

It is not possible for everyone to get professional counseling or afford a lengthy series of counseling sessions. Many have asked the question, "Why do we need so many counselors today?" I'm not sure there is justification for the number of professional counselors we have today, but it is my observation that because we are such a transient society, the support systems once available to us (parents, grandparents, uncles, aunts, etc.) are no longer in place.

The extended family was at one time available, because of a close proximity of residence, to support and give advice to a young couple in reference to marriage and parenting. The rural communities in America have shrunk since World War II and for many families such support systems are not available to a great degree. Thus, there is more reliance on professionally trained counselors.

The church is in a position to take up the slack in this area and is capable of providing the advice and counsel necessary to support families and individuals who are having serious problems in their relationships with people and with God (Romans 15:14). The church should provide resources for members who need to develop counseling and communicating skills to reach out to hurting people.

This book is being offered as a resource for Skilled Helpers, who are leaders in the church, and the workplace, for the purpose of developing people skills in order to assist others dealing with life's everyday problems. We refer to the Bible as the ultimate source of authority and with the realization that only God has the answers to our problems because He is the Great Creator.

The study of psychology is a valid pursuit. The term "psychology" refers to the study of the mind, and since God created the mind, it is as important to study the laws that apply to it, as it is to study the laws that apply to the body in physiology.

Anything God has created has, by definition, laws that apply to it. Skilled Helpers should be aware of these laws in order to make sound judgments in reference to the violations of such laws and their consequences.

Skilled Helpers also need to realize that they cannot help everyone and some people will not respond positively to their efforts. When the people we try to help are willing to put forth the effort and grow, it can be very rewarding for the Skilled Helper and a positive result for the spiritual and emotional health of the people he/she helps (Proverbs 15:22).

Being a Skilled Helper involves more than diagnosing a problem, it also involves supporting, confronting and directing a hurting person through the healing process. Only God can supply the answers needed in these areas. We do not believe in "non-directive" counseling or "guilt-ridden" therapy.

We do believe in a God who confronts us in our sins, forgives us when we repent, and loves us unconditionally. We believe in the power of prayer and that God responds to our needs when we sincerely come to Him in submission to His will (I John 5:14, 15).

Chapter One

THE POWER OF THE MIND

The power of the mind continues to amaze even the casual observer. The brain is much like a computer. It has access to a personal library of thousands of thoughts and pictures, ready to expose them on the imaginary monitor screen in our heads at a moment's notice. The mind can recall, at will, any programmed belief system that is in that personal library. Some of the belief systems are true and some are false.

The brain does amazing things but appears unable to distinguish the difference between a truth and a lie. If a person believes that something is true, the brain will accept it as truth. All that is required is repetition of that belief for the brain to record it as truth for all time. Just like a computer's hard drive, whatever you have saved in your mind will stay there until you change it.

Most belief systems are formed in childhood. Once accepted, these beliefs are recorded as true even if they are not. "Belief Systems" then, are those collections of beliefs that the brain has recorded (after much repetition) and recalls at will because we use them when needed and believe them to be true. These belief systems have a direct relationship to how we see our world and how we think our world sees us.

Cognitive Therapy

Many social scientists and psychologists today have concentrated their research on what is commonly called Cognitive Therapy. The word "cognitive" refers to the thought processes we all have, whether they are words we tell ourselves or fantasies and dreams. Two psychologists that have been the main contributors to this research are Albert Ellis (1962) and A. T. Beck (1979).

Cognitive therapy typically proceeds in three stages: (1) The presentation of the cognitive concept, (2) The process of awareness of dysfunctional thoughts on the part of the counselee and (3) The rejection of the dysfunctional thoughts and the substitution of more functional thinking.

I believe this therapy process (with the Bible as a final source of authority) is much more effective than the Psychodynamic (Freud) and Behavioral (Skinner) therapies that have been more popular with social scientists in the past. The concept of changing behavior by changing the thought processes (or beliefs) is basic to Christian conversion and living.

The apostle Paul established this concept as God ordained when he said, "Do not conform any longer to the pattern of this world, but be transformed by the renewing of your mind" (Romans 12:2). The Bible emphasizes that we should control our thoughts and imaginations (Philippians 4:8). Two Christian psychologists, who have given a more biblical emphasis to this theory, are Dr. William Backus ("Telling Yourself The Truth") and Dr. Chris Thurman ("The Lies We Believe").

There is a danger that cognitive change can be constructed in a very superficial manner. Beck and others emphasize the need to get down to the "core beliefs" (belief systems) of the counselee, where a major effort is devoted to developing a self-awareness of "what we tell ourselves."

Albert Ellis has identified a number of irrational beliefs that are a part of our self-talk (Ellis and Grieger 1977). The following are commonly held self-destructive beliefs:

1. I need to be loved by everyone.
2. It is terrible when things are not precisely the way I want them.
3. Painful things that happen to me are due to circumstances or other people outside of my control.
4. I need to get upset about threatening things and focus all my attention on them.
5. It is better to avoid my problems than to face them.
6. I must be totally competent in every situation.
7. If something at one time has affected my life, it will always affect me.
8. I must be completely self-controlled.
9. Doing little or nothing about a situation will make me happy.
10. I cannot control my emotions and need not assume responsibility for how I feel.
11. There is always a right and perfect solution; there will be a catastrophe if I cannot identify it.[1]

There certainly are other lies that can be identified, but I believe that Ellis has captured the essence of the negative thoughts we believe about ourselves. These belief systems create in us a potential series of "perceived threats" that we allow to control our feelings and behavior. Even if the belief systems are lies, if we believe them to be true, they can be acted upon as true and become "self-destructive lies" that cause us to make wrong choices in our lives.

These belief systems then cause us to perceive things as threats, whether real or imaginary, and threats cause us to get angry. Since anger is a defense mechanism, we react to many perceived threats automatically, often causing a lot of heartaches and problems in our interpersonal relationships.

Our reaction to perceived threats are automatic and programmed in our brain. We learned such automatic reactions to threats from the angry behavior of significant people in our lives when we were children and because certain temperaments are prone to different anger responses. We usually do not challenge these responses. They become automatic like driving a car.

When we first learned how to drive a car, we were unsure of the depth perception and the use of the pedals, shifting gears and steering, etc. After several tries, we repeated the information on how to drive often enough that the brain recorded it as a programmed response. That is why those of us who learned how to drive do it now automatically without thinking about it. The brain has the ability to record those belief systems in our subconscious mind and they will stay there until we challenge them with another belief system.

If we were to drive in England, we would quickly realize that driving over there is different than in America. We must now drive on the left-hand side of the road and the steering wheel is on the right-hand side of the car. After repeatedly telling our brain that we are learning new information about depth perception, etc., it will finally override the old information and now subconsciously recall the new. Such programming is necessary for the changing of the subconscious mind.

This is why belief systems are the most important factors in our "mental" and "emotional" life. They determine what we see as positive and negative in our lives. They determine what we perceive as threats in our lives and therefore our "feelings" and "actions" as well.

How Do We Find The Truth?

Great thinkers and scholars over the centuries have attempted to define "truth," what it is and what it means in our lives. When Jesus told Pilate, during His trial before him, "... I came into the world to testify to the truth," Pilate responded by asking, "What is truth?" Earlier Jesus had said, "... you will know the truth, and the truth will set you free" (John 8:32; 18:37-38). I realize that Jesus was referring to truth about God and our relationship to Him, but I also believe that all truth will set us free from the lies that enslave us emotionally, spiritually and psychologically. God's word is truth (John 17:17; II Timothy 3:16,17).

The only other standard for truth is "reality." I realize that this standard can be subjective, but we must be rational in our thinking in all situations before us. The Bible doesn't address everything specifically. If our understanding of reality does not contradict the Bible, it can be a logical standard for truth, although it must at times be relative in its application.

Lies destroy three things in our lives: (1) Identity, (2) Values and (3) Relationships. When we tell ourselves lies, we redefine what we are and we tend to try to be somebody else and it causes emotional dissonance and creates in us the propensity to
make bad choices. Lies also destroy our values because we lose sight of the proper distinction between good choices and bad choices. The lies we tell ourselves about our self-worth also destroy relationships because we are tempted to be too sensitive to rejection and many times make bad choices to avoid it.

Some of what we tell ourselves is not in word form. Our thoughts are often images or attitudes without words attached to them. You may feel uncomfortable and isolated in crowded places but never actually put these feelings into words. You may be fearful of a thing and avoid it without really knowing what's going on in your belief systems at all.

It is not, however, events either past or present, which make us feel the way we feel, but our "interpretation" of those events. Therefore, our belief systems are a product of what we tell ourselves about our environment. It is not our circumstances that cause us to have negative feelings but our interpretation of those circumstances.

The apostle Paul refused to allow circumstances to dictate his feelings or behavior when he said, "... I have learned to be content whatever the circumstances" (Philippians 4:11). He refused to allow a Roman prison to

feeling of smug self-satisfaction

diminish his joy and faith in Christ Jesus (Philippians 4:4-7). We often allow our interpretation of events (filtered through our belief systems) to determine how we are going to feel at any given moment. Paul was not equating "contentment" with "complacency." Our joy and contentment are often dependent upon what we tell ourselves about our circumstances. Sometimes we tell ourselves the lie, "I can't change the way I am." If we believe this lie, we won't even try to change it.

Childhood memories are not always what we would like them to be and we are not always capable of interpreting them correctly. God planned that we should be born without knowledge of anything. We do have some instinctual propensities such as desiring to eat, walk, talk, etc. When we are born we are without knowledge of who we are and what our world is like. We are born with the desire to develop a self-concept, either a positive or negative one. Since our minds are basically a blank slate when we are born, we learn about ourselves, and what our world is like from our interpretation of the events in our life.

Dr. William Backus, a clinical psychologist, says in his best selling book, 'Telling Yourself The Truth' that, "We began thinking the way we now think at some time or another in our lives and often our thoughts and beliefs originate in childhood." He also says that, "Some of the primitive beliefs and behaviors that cause our unpleasant feelings and maladaptive behavior as adults were acquired in our early years."[2]

Billy's Story

The following story is true of so many people whom I have counseled, who have troubled lives from which the source can be traced to their childhood. Billy was 45 years old and on the verge of a divorce and had a drinking problem. That was the "presenting" problem, which is many times not the "primary" problem. Billy had a long history of verbally abusing his wife and it was revealed that he spent most of his time with his parents trying to restore some kind of relationship with them. He wanted them to confirm that they loved him.

During Billy's childhood he believed that his parents didn't love him because he didn't receive any hugs, expressions of love or verbal appreciation for his accomplishments. All his parents seemed to do was to criticize him. He would come home with a report card with three A's, two B's and a C, and his parents would concentrate on the C, giving him verbal rebukes for it.

There didn't seem to be anything he could do to be accepted by them. Billy repeated statements to himself such as, "my parents don't love me" and later on in his childhood, when he could think in abstract terms, he would extend the lie to the point of believing that he was unlovable.

Billy had so programmed his mind to believe he was unloved that he transferred the anger he felt for his parents to his wife and began to drink to avoid the empty feeling of being unloved by his parents. He then spent a great deal of time trying to get them to show any indication that they loved him, even to the point of neglecting his family.

The ironic thing about this story is that, after interviewing his parents, it was evident his parents did love him. They had believed that parenting required stern measures and that expressing love and appreciation would only weaken the child. They feared that as an adult he would not be able to face a hard and difficult world. In both cases, lies were programmed in the brain through repetition and from those lies interpretations were made that ultimately caused dysfunctional feelings and behavior in their lives.

Billy and his parents had to recognize the lies they had been telling themselves and remove them and replace them with the truth. When that was accomplished, Billy realized his parents did love him and he began to deal with his anger in a biblical way. The problems in his marriage and his drinking were resolved and he began to live a life of hope.

Billy's problem was that he had interpreted the behavior of his parents as rejection. His parents had interpreted the purpose of parenting as a means of hardening a child to deal with the world rather than expressing the love, acceptance and appropriate discipline Billy needed to face the world with a sense of security and confidence. Billy also came to know the Lord and through much prayer and Bible study he became a believer in the power of God's word. I moved from that city shortly after this, and I can't help but believe that Billy was eventually baptized and became faithful to the Lord. The power of God's word in dealing with man's everyday problems never ceases to amaze me.

Runaway Jane

In the movie, "Runaway Bride" starring Richard Gere and Julia Roberts, the main story line was about a young woman who had been engaged many times. Every time she reached the altar, she became so fearful of committing to the vows of marriage that she bolted from the church building and ran away, leaving the bridegroom with a stunned and embarrassed look on his face. Such behavior becomes a programmed response to a perceived threat and is very predictable.

One day a woman came into my counseling office appearing very depressed and without hope. Jane shared a story similar to the movie "Runaway Bride." She had been engaged several times but each time the wedding day drew near, she and her fiancé would begin fighting until eventually the engagement would be called off. Jane asked the question, "Why do my relationships with men end close to the time we are about to get married?" I told her that her story was certainly interesting and then I proceeded to ask questions about her relationship with her father.

I have found that many women experience similar situations with men. Experimental evidence has shown that these women most likely did not have a healthy, nurturing relationship with their fathers. Jane told me that her father deserted the family when she was eight years old. His departure was very traumatic for her and she blamed herself for his leaving. Her mother tried to explain that it wasn't her fault, but she could not accept the truth. Jane was an only child who adored her father and thought that he loved her. She never got over the deep disappointment and self-inflicted blame for his desertion. She would never see or hear from her father again.

After many counseling sessions, it became apparent that Jane had convinced herself that men would reject and desert her because her father did. She had repeated this lie so often that her subconscious mind finally accepted it.

Jane told me that each time a relationship became serious, she would find something wrong with her fiancé and eventually they would fight and split up. It became evident that she had accepted the lies she told herself and that her mind was literally bringing about what is called a "Self-fulfilling Prophecy." She would subconsciously torpedo the relationship, fearing her fiancé would reject her after marriage. She would end the relationship before such a thing could happen to her again. She suffered from programmed lies that destroyed her relationships and caused her emotional and psychological pain.

Through counseling, Jane began to understand how the mind is programmed and that the lies she was telling herself, though she believed them to be true, were causing her emotional distress.

After several sessions, Jane was able to recognize the lies, remove them, and replace them with the truth. She began to heal and eventually was able to develop a relationship with a man that led to marriage. It's been proven to me that the Bible teaches powerful truths that give our life purpose.

The Therapeutic Process

There is a comfortable sequence in counseling that differs with each individual. Hurrying information out of people destroys the therapeutic process, which is so vital in helping them gain insights.

After the counselee has taken the first step in seeking help with a problem, the next step is to feel comfortable about discussing it. But in this desirable therapeutic process he does not talk about just any part of the problem. He selects, session by session, those segments which are easiest for him to think about and discuss. He may not realize it, but he does not want the counselor to disrupt the succession, which he chooses for revealing information. In fact, he may not know what he is going to reveal, but during the session various aspects of his problem emerge naturally. Each aspect comes at the right time for him. The counselor realizes that by remaining a catalytic agent, he allows this process to evidence itself.

At this point the counselor may actually do harm by pulling out or insisting upon certain information and insights which are not timed to the counselee's own readiness. The counselor does not know what the order of the process should be. Neither can he know beforehand because it differs from person to person. However, he should be sensitive to the process, which is taking place and not cause confusion by pulling certain information or forcing insights ahead of their natural emergence. If he does create disorder in the natural arrangement of the counselee's revealing information, the counselee will, possibly unconsciously, resent it and feel frustrated.

This natural "coming out" or presentation of the problem relieves the counselee from the tension of self-consciousness. It also enables him to feel at ease about hearing himself say what he does. He is not fearful of what he has said; neither does he regret having verbalized it, because it came without force or coercion.

The next logical step in the therapeutic process is the counselee's desire to carefully think and talk through each part of the material he has presented. He senses that merely "saying" it, is not adequate enough to comprehend the problem. It must be handled and examined if it is to result in clearer understanding and eventual effectiveness. The impulses which bind him must be loosened a strand at a time, and each one requires its own scrutiny and disposal. So he discusses each point in detail.

As the counselee comes face to face with each force that has combined to make him feel and act as he does, he begins to entertain, at least verbally, new ways of reacting to old problems. He thinks of ways to overcome his problems. He rationalizes new steps to take. But his willingness to do this depends largely upon the counselor's skill in aiding, rather than disrupting the natural therapeutic process. If things have been upset and tangled, the counselee will find it difficult to think of or earnestly follow a reasonable program of rehabilitation.

Many people coming to a counselor are readily advised what to do in order to improve. But the counselee finds it difficult to follow something for which he is not prepared. If, on the other hand, the counselor carefully leads the counselee to the place where, in his own readiness, he can see likely solutions, he will be more apt to accept and begin following them.

The Benefits of Cognitive Therapy

Cognitive therapy usually lasts between ten and twenty sessions. Of course, with any therapy, this varies a great deal depending on the nature of the counselee's emotional difficulties and resources. Occasionally a counselee will show significant improvement after two or three sessions, and sometimes, cognitive therapy continues for a year or more.

Unlike some short-term therapies, cognitive therapy focuses on past events as well as present symptoms. In his book, "Cognitive Therapy and the Emotional Disorders," psychiatrist Aaron Beck describes similarities between cognitive therapy and psychodynamic therapy, a long-term method emphasizing insight into childhood experiences. In both forms of therapy, the counselee is asked to introspect and develop insight regarding thoughts, feelings, and wishes. Both forms attempt to reorganize personality rather than just remove symptoms. Both forms of therapy also require the counselee to work through maladaptive beliefs and arrive at more healthy ways of thinking.

However, one of the significant differences between psychodynamic and cognitive therapies is the time required for treatment. Psychodynamic therapists often work for a year or more with their counselees, sometimes meeting two or more times per week. Cognitive therapy is much briefer.

Cognitive therapy is based on the theory that our thought processes are the cause of our maladaptive behavior. Psychodynamic therapy, as Sigmund Freud designed it, is based on the sexual and aggressive drives of man as a species resulting from the processes of evolution.

To the Christian counselor, it is important that the therapy chosen as a means of helping others be based on the belief that man is a created being and that God has the answers to his problems.

Christian Counseling

A counselor is not Christian merely by virtue of being anti-Freudian or anti-humanistic psychology, but we would also argue that a counselor is not thoroughly Christian merely by virtue of throwing around a few Bible verses. None of the existing counseling theories, (religious or non-religious) adequately plumb the depths of the complexity of human character and of the change process.

There are many theoretical options open to counselors who desire to be distinctively Christian in what they do. Christian counselors may operate differently from each other.

But we would argue that there will be or should be certain commonalities across all counselors who are attempting to be distinctly Christian. The basis for these commonalities is the special claim the gospel has on the counseling process compared to work in other vocations, such as medicine, accounting or construction. We agree with Christian critics of psychology such as Jay Adams, who say that the counseling processes are of such a nature that they must be thoroughly reconstructed from a biblical foundation to lay claim to the title "Christian Counseling."

Actually, no one should be better qualified to counsel than the true disciple of God. He/she should have accurate insight into human nature. True wisdom and understanding emanate from God. Through His Word, the believer finds the answers to life's problems. Not only that, he has the powerful resources of prayer. As he grows in grace and in the knowledge of his Lord and Savior, Jesus Christ, he develops an attractive personality that radiates Christ.

To be good counselors we must be the right kind of people ourselves. We must let the Lord take charge of our lives. When we do, we will have the "wisdom that is from above" (James 3:13-18). This wisdom is first "pure." It is not tainted by worldliness or selfish gain. It is not contaminated by our own faulty wisdom. It is sound and right and righteous! It comes from God. Everyone gives advice; but much of it is far from right and pure. The Bible teaches that those who help others should be spiritual (Galatians 6:1).

A Christian counselor is to live righteously so that he will have pure wisdom. His wisdom is to be peaceable. Some people have the right answers but the wrong attitude. We do not help people by arguing with them. We only set up walls of resentment. Peace is a rare quality. You look in vain to find it among nations and you rarely see it in individuals. You do find it in some Christians; but regrettably, too few. God's Word teaches us to be peaceful (Matthew 5:9).

Peace is the result of confessed and forgiven sin. The Christian counselor must be a disciple who readily recognizes his own sins and confesses to the Lord and shares these weaknesses and needs with a confidant (James 5:16) who can give support and help him be accountable. Sometimes it seems easier to hide or excuse sin than to ask God's forgiveness.

A Christian counselor must know how to engage in practicing dealing with sin in his own life before he can be effective in helping others deal with theirs. Paul said, "Brethren, even if a man is caught in a trespass, you who are spiritual, restore such a one in a spiritual of gentleness, each one looking to yourself, lest you too be tempted" (Galatians 6:1 NASB).

Review Questions

1. What do we mean by "belief systems?"
2. What is "Cognitive Therapy?"
3. How would you define "perceived threats?"
4. What sources do we use to find "truth?"
5. Who is Albert Ellis?
6. How would you define "Self-Fulfilling Prophecy?"
7. Who are the two Christian psychologists who redefined Cognitive Therapy in Christian terms?
8. How had Billy interpreted his parent's behavior towards him?

Chapter Two

THE POWER OF SELF-TALK

You don't have to be a professional counselor to be competent to counsel. There must be a desire to help people, with knowledge of the Bible. These qualities and an understanding of how the mind works, can prepare you to be an effective counselor.

In his book "Competent to Counsel," Jay Adams emphasizes the fact that a Christian, who has such a knowledge of the Bible, can be effective in helping change the lives of those who are hurting and in need of support. The apostle Paul says, "I myself am convinced, my brothers, that you yourselves are full of goodness, complete in knowledge and competent to instruct one another" (Romans 15:14). Adams points out that the Greek word for "instruct" (or "admonish" in K.J.V.) in this passage is "noutheteo," which implies confrontation.

This word is also used in a passage that commands confronting by teaching through singing to one another (Colossians 3:16). W. E. Vine says that "noutheteo" is used of "instruction," of "warning."[3] Adams has emphasized that the word "counsel" (if it includes confronting) would fulfill the true meaning of the word "noutheteo." Of course the implication is that a Christian would be qualified if he/she were full of goodness and knowledge of the word of God. Such a person would then be qualified to speak the truth in love, using God's word to confront and counsel others (Ephesians 4:15, 16). There are certain psychological problems that a professional Christian counselor would need to address and these will be discussed later in this chapter.

The first thing we must understand as counselors is that we can control our mindset but don't usually try. The apostle Paul tells us to control our thoughts and realize the power of them. He tells us that we should think on those things that are truthful and positive in our lives (Philippians 4:8).

We also need to control our imaginations. We often imagine and fantasize about things that are unhealthy for us spiritually, emotionally, and psychologically. Paul tells us that we can bring our thoughts into obedience to and agreement with the knowledge of Christ (II Corinthians 10:5). The word of God is the standard of truth in this text and anything that contradicts it in our thinking must be subdued and rejected, if we want to live a functional and faithful life in Christ.

Biblical principles come from God and they apply to every facet of our lives. "The mind of sinful man is death, but the mind controlled by the Spirit is life and peace" (Romans 8:6). Thoughts determine the heart and the mindset of sinful man, and change must come first from those thoughts.

The wisdom of God supersedes the wisdom of man. Again the apostle Paul said, "Where is the wise man? Where is the scholar? Where is the philosopher of this age? Has not God made foolish the wisdom of the world" (I Corinthians 1:20)?

Dealing With Self-Talk

One of my favorite stories is about the worker on a construction job in the city, who hurt his hand. He went to the job foreman and showed him his injury. The foreman looked at it and said it appeared he needed medical attention and suggested he go to a nearby clinic and have it looked at. Upon entering the front doors of the clinic he noticed two more doors. A sign over one door said "emergency" and the sign over the other door said "appointment." He thought for a moment and decided that it was an emergency and went through that door. Inside he found two more doors, one said "injury" and the other "illness." Because he had an injury, he went through the "injury" door. Once again he found two more doors, one said "internal" and the other "external." He was becoming a little frustrated but decided to go through the "external" door and found two more doors. One said "major" and the other "minor." He was reasonably sure it was a minor injury, so he passed through the "minor" door and found himself out on the street. He went back to the construction site, whereupon the foreman asked him how it went. The worker shook his head and said, "Well they didn't help me much but they sure were organized!"

This may be a hypothetical story, but it reveals a lot about human nature. When we have problems in life, we too often focus on changing our feelings and/or behavior instead of addressing the thoughts (or "self-talk"), which are most often the problem. We often try to control our feelings and behavior and get everything organized so that we can solve what we think is the problem, and in doing so, we lose sight of the real problem.

I am convinced that most of our behavior is preceded by feelings, which are preceded by thoughts. If I were to use the analogy of "disease" vs. "symptoms," the disease would be the thoughts and the symptoms would be the feelings and behavior. We would quickly change doctors if the one we were seeing treated only the symptoms and not the disease. This illustrates how important it is to challenge our thoughts when we are having strong feelings that create problems or when we are engaging in self-destructive behavior.

"Self-talk" refers to the words we tell ourselves in our thoughts. It is what we say to ourselves all the time about how we see ourselves, how we perceive our world and how we think our world sees us.

A "self-destructive belief" is a lie that we tell ourselves and we believe it. It is a lie or a series of lies, programmed into a belief system that we have come to believe as true over a period of time. When we wonder why we feel the way we do, this should be our first warning sign that something is wrong with our belief systems. Dr. Backus, in his book, states that such lies are "the direct cause of emotional turmoil, maladaptive behavior and most so-called 'mental illness.'"[4] Phrases such as "I _always_ make mistakes" or "I'm _never_ going to be loved by anyone" are good examples of absolute statements. We will believe these lies when something happens in our life that is negative and the brain recalls them automatically. Our self-talk has a power and a hold over us that is not truly appreciated or realized. We seldom challenge our self-talk, because we have a tendency as human beings to accept it as truth.

Beware of Absolutes

Absolute statements, in the majority of cases, are lies we tell ourselves to release us from the responsibility of dealing with an issue or a problem. We can recognize absolute statements by the absolute words, such as: "never," "always," "everybody," "can't," "must," "nobody," and "forever," etc. Absolute statements do not allow for exceptions or variables. They are statements that are automatically believed and rarely do we challenge their truthfulness. Some absolute statements can be true, such as, "I'll never be a rocket scientist" or "I can't see myself as a professional athlete."

In our conversations with others and our self-talk we, for the most part, use absolute statements as lies that help release us from our responsibilities. If we believe such statements about ourselves, we set ourselves up for negative feelings, low self-worth and self-destructive behavior.

I believe that negative and distorted statements people tell themselves are from Satan (Acts 5:3; John 8:44; II Corinthians 11:14). The mind accepts these statements without question and then, like poison in our system, these lies corrupt our belief systems and we make bad choices and create painful, emotional consequences. Like a computer "virus," these lies kill us spiritually, emotionally, psychologically and mentally. If God is telling us, "Do not let any unwholesome talk come out of your mouths, but only what is helpful for building others up according to their needs, that it may benefit those who listen," doesn't this principle also apply to our self-talk (Ephesians 4:29)?

I'm sure we could all find something about our lives we would like to change. No one's life circumstances are perfect. But what are we telling ourselves about these circumstances? If we want to have the JOY in our lives that God has promised us, we need to reject the lies we tell ourselves and replace them with the truth (Philippians 4:4-13). Our circumstances may not change but our "belief systems" can change and make a difference. Feelings are inherently neither "good" nor "bad," they're just feelings. The thoughts that cause negative feelings, and ultimately bad behavior, must be changed, and once they are changed, the feelings will follow.

Beauty is in the Eye of the Beholder

Betty came into my office one day very depressed. She was 24 years old and confessed that she was seriously considering taking her life. She said she was tired of being used by men and that she couldn't find a man who would simply love her for who she was without being used by him. Her two brothers had sexually abused her from the time she was 14 years old until she left home at 17. She told her mother a year or so after the abuse began what was happening, but her mother would not believe her. Her brothers forced her to have sex with them every afternoon after school. After several counseling sessions she revealed to me that her uncle, who lived nearby, had sexually abused her from the age of 6 until she was 12 years old. Over the years she had come to believe that all men would want from her was sex. She had told herself this lie during her formative years and by the time she came to me she was convinced that it was the truth.

Betty was very beautiful and many men were attracted to her. The interesting thing about her story was that, as an adult on her own, she would select certain men, who were on the make, and have a one-night stand with them and then would look for the next one to come along. As a clerk in a hotel, she only had eyes for the men who would abuse and use her.

Betty had so programmed herself that she couldn't imagine falling in love with a man, who would respect and love her and be responsible. In fact, she couldn't even see herself being attracted to such a man. She was only attracted to the ones who were obviously promiscuous. After several weeks of cognitive therapy, Betty was able to recognize that her problems were a result of the lies she told herself.

The very men in Betty's life, who should have loved and protected her, had instead abused her. She needed to see that her programmed belief system, of how she perceived men, came from her interpretation of these experiences, not from the experiences themselves. She began to accept the fact that she could control and change the interpretations but not the experiences. The trauma of being sexually abused would not be forgotten. The pain would be lessened in the future as she learned to replace the lies she was telling herself with the truth.

Recognizing, Removing and Replacing

There are certain steps a leader can take when dealing with someone who has a serious problem and is asking for counsel. Whether you are a church leader, business leader, or a father/mother in the home, you can use these principles to help others. In order to be an effective counselor you must first discover the lies in your own belief systems and replace them with the truth.

There must be the willingness, on the counselor's part, as well as the counselee's, to confront beliefs that are causing trouble in personal relationships. You must recognize the behavior in your life that is self-destructive or damaging to relationships. Because "feelings" are a symptom of what we are thinking, they should be dealt with first. I usually ask my counselees to write down in a journal on a daily basis the disruptive feelings they experienced and the events that caused them. From this journal I am able to see a pattern of feelings during certain circumstances and reflect on the possible beliefs that counselees might have that are lies and are affecting their behavior. We then make a chart with the counselee writing down the possible lies on one side and the possible truth statements on the other. Every potential counselor should go through this exercise for himself/herself to find out what possible lies might be behind any behavior that is dysfunctional.

If a counselee does not believe in an absolute standard of truth, there is not much of a basis for effective counseling. When counseling Betty, it was necessary to confront her about her behavior and get her to recognize that sex outside of marriage is sinful, according to the word of God. She had to recognize, not only that such behavior was sinful, but that it caused her problems in her relationships. She had to recognize "right" from "wrong" and that God's word is the absolute standard to go by. Once Betty recognized and accepted God's word as the final authority, she then reached a point in our counseling when she could truly recognize the lies she was telling herself.

Once we have learned to recognize the lies, we must remove them from our subconscious mind. One of the steps required of my counselees is that they set aside 10 to 15 minutes each morning to review their statements of lies and truths and pray about them, asking God to help them remove the lies from their memory and replace them with the truth statements. This process did two things for Betty: It helped her to "red flag" her lies during the day when she would have a tendency to fall back on them when something happened that prompted the brain to recall them automatically; and it also allowed God to be involved in the process of answering prayer and giving her the wisdom and peace that only He can give (Philippians 4:6,7; James 1:5-8). This is the same process that a person goes through when he/she is converted to the Lord. Paul said, "You were taught, with regard to your former way of life, to put off your old self, which is being corrupted by its deceitful desires; to be made new in the attitude of your minds; and to put on the new self, created to be like God in true righteousness and holiness" (Ephesians 4:22-24).

Before we were converted to Christ, we believed lies such as: "I don't need Christ right now" or "God doesn't exist" or "I must be perfect to become a Christian," etc. When we finally decided we needed Christ in our lives, we began to recognize the lies we were telling ourselves and began removing them and replacing them with the truth. The step of replacing lies with the truth may take some time and we have to be willing to be patient and let the process be completed.

We need to practice telling ourselves truth statements in place of the lies for as long as it takes for it to become as natural as breathing or driving a car. The old saying, "practice makes perfect" is powerful. When Paul told those who were liars to tell the truth, he didn't simply tell them to stop lying, he told them they needed to become "tellers of truth." He told those who were thieves that not only should they stop stealing, but that they must find gainful employment and give to those in need (Ephesians 4:25-28). The principle in this passage is that we must put into practice the things we believe.

A Sample List

SELF-DESTRUCTIVE LIES	BIBLICAL TRUTH STATEMENTS
I am lonely	I may be alone but I'm not lonely as long as I have the Lord – James 4:6-10
I'm dumb	Thank you Lord for giving me the ability to think – Philippians 4:8
I'm miserable	I can be content in the Lord – Philippians 4:6-12
Nobody loves me	God loves me – John 3:16
Nobody cares about me	God cares – I Peter 5:7
I can't go on any longer	I can do all things through Christ – Philippians 4:13
I must be perfect	All have sinned and fallen short of the glory of God – Romans 3:23
I never do anything right	Thank you Lord for giving me the ability to do some things well – Romans 12:3-8
I must always please people	I need to have the heart of a servant to serve God, not to please men – Ephesians 6:6-8

A Criteria For Making Referrals

When should a Skilled Helper refer a person who needs help, to another counselor or someone with more expertise in the counseling profession? This is an important question. I do not want to give the impression in this book that if the reader just follows these guidelines for counseling, he/she will qualify as a professional counselor.

A counselor is considered a professional when he/she has a degree on the level of a Masters or Doctorate in Counseling Psychology or a related field and has developed the expertise in counseling through experience. The following cases should be referred:

1. When a counselee has expressed definite psychotic tendencies, such as: hallucinations, incoherence, paranoia or erratic behavior.
2. When a combination of two or more symptoms of clinical depression are observed, such as: insomnia nearly every day, eating irregularities, severe apathy, suicide ideation, continuous depressive moods, significant weight loss or weight gain, diminished ability to think or susceptibility to disease.
3. When a counselee has excessive mood swings suggesting a Bi-polar or a Manic-Depressive condition.
4. When a hormonal imbalance is detected by a doctor or qualified medical person.
5. In all cases that apparently require a medical doctor's attention.
6. In cases of abuse such as: sexual, physical, substance, etc., where professionals with the expertise and qualifications are better able to handle such cases.
7. When the counselee has made previous suicide attempts or threats.
8. When the counselee expresses uncontrollable anger or threats of violence.
9. In cases of extreme anxiety/panic or eating disorders.
10. In all cases where it is apparent that you are unsuccessful in helping the counselee to progress towards complete mental and emotional health.

No Skilled Helper should be ashamed to admit that a case is beyond his/her expertise and should be referred to a professional. It requires of us that we put a person's best interests at the forefront and our concern should be for his/her health, not our reputation. Our credibility as Skilled Helpers rests on a person's acceptance of us as caring people. There are questions at this point every counselor should ask himself:

1. What is the context of the problem?
2. Who are the persons involved?
3. What environmental factors are contributing to the difficulty?
4. What is my motive for counseling this person?

The Role of The Skilled Helper

The Skilled Helper's goal is to help the counselee find solutions to his/her problems and help him/her experience healing. The Skilled Helper cannot solve a person's problems, but can help. The counselee must work at and finally discover what she/he must do to find a solution, never leaving God out of the process.

The Skilled Helper looks for clues into the motives behind the question(s) asked by the counselee, in order to gain insight into the problem and direct the counselee toward a solution. Many times a counselee will present a problem to the counselor, but give signals that there is a more pressing problem that he/she is struggling with.

The Skilled Helper's attitude is vitally important to the counselee. When a counselor is kind, the counselee feels cared for and comforted and realizes someone understands how he/she feels. The counselee is seeking (often unconsciously) a counselor with poise and composure. The Skilled Helper must realize that objectivity is seldom achieved through a close identification with the counselee or his/her problem.

The following are ways to avoid involvement in the counselee's problems:

1. Commit the problem to the Lord (James 1:5-8).
2. Do not officially counsel close friends, relatives or co-workers.
3. Do not get involved in orchestrating a counselee's personal life.
4. Do not touch a counselee in inappropriate ways.
5. Do not become emotionally involved with the counselee beyond a caring mode.
6. Focus attention on the counseling process.

All forms of counseling require counselees to become students of their own weaknesses and needs. Those who profit the most from counseling, including cognitive therapy, are those who are able to look accurately at their thoughts, feelings, motives, and desires.

Some people come to counseling with good insight. They are able to understand and describe their thoughts and feelings with ease. They come from environments where feelings are openly discussed or they have participated in counseling before. These counselees are usually able to progress quickly in cognitive therapy. Once they understand the relationship between self-talk and feelings, they learn to monitor their thoughts and find alternative ways of thinking to control their feelings.

Others come for counseling with poorer skills of insight. They know they feel bad, but they don't know how to describe their feelings carefully nor do they understand the relationship between their thoughts and their feelings. This is especially common for male counselees who have not been socialized to understand or express their feelings in our current culture.

When it comes to our self-talk, we need the Word of God to free us from our unhealthy beliefs and allow us to see God more accurately. God's love – perhaps the only true unconditional love – can meet our deepest emotional needs. The apostle Paul instructed the Christians at Rome to not conform to the ways of the world, but to be "transformed by the renewing of your mind" (Romans 12:2).

The transformation Paul describes allows us to see the world through a different set of eyes – eyes that seek God's truth above personal comfort or pleasure. The goal of cognitive therapy is similar. Cognitive counselors help their counselees identify and change core beliefs, to trade in their old set of eyes for a new set that can interpret the world more accurately. In reaching this goal, counselees learn to employ skills of insight, inductive reasoning, experimentation, and repetition.

The Responsibility of Leaders

As leaders in some capacity, God is expecting us to be honorable in that role and to act like Christians at all times, both in attitude and action. In all cases we must have the mind of Christ and hold the counselee's interests above our own (Philippians 2:3-8).

Review Questions

1. How would you define "the power of self-talk?"
2. What do we mean by the term "absolute statements?"
3. How does the three-step process deal with self-destructive lies?
4. What are three cases that should be referred to a professional counselor?
5. What are the four questions that a counselor should ask himself?
6. Why is "objectivity" so important?
7. Why shouldn't a Skilled Helper be embarrassed when referring a counselee to another counselor?
8. What is the responsibility of leaders when it comes to counseling their followers?

Chapter Three

THE POWER OF SELF-CONTROL

The power of self-control depends on our ability to realize the power of the mind. We live in a society where people easily play the blame game and claim to be victims. It is too easy to blame others, things, the weather or God for the lack of self-control we have in our lives. We can control our emotions if we want to; it is within our ability to do so. The Bible states emphatically that we can and must learn to control our emotions.

The apostle Paul tells us that, "the fruit of the Spirit is love, joy, peace, patience, kindness, goodness, faithfulness, gentleness and self-control" (Galatians 5:22). The first step in developing self-control is to realize that we have such control, if we have the will to exercise it. God would never command us to do something that we have not the ability to do. A case in point is the problem of depression.

Many depressed people can begin to get over depression when they begin to take responsibility for their feelings. By putting themselves in charge of their own lives they can begin to get better. In their popular book, "Happiness Is a Choice," Dr. Frank Minirth and Dr. Paul Meier, who are both respected psychiatrists, based their book on the premise that depression is a choice of the will and can be controlled.

I happen to believe that the main cause of depression, in most cases, is the negative self-talk that some people engage in that eventually leads them to the point when they lose hope. If at this point a person does not deal with his/her depression, it can develop to what is called "Clinical Depression."

Clinical Depression is a state where there is a severe chemical imbalance in the brain and if diagnosed properly by a physician, can be treated effectively with anti-depressants. In such a case, the ability of a person to deal with the depression without appropriate drugs is very difficult, but we should not lose hope (I Thessalonians 4:13).

Depression is a choice in many cases though, and it comes about when a person chooses to be a victim of their emotions instead of developing a mindset of self-control. In depression, the worse we feel, the less we do.

Then our lack of activity causes us to feel guilt and sadness over our passivity, and we get even further depressed.

The truth is when we take control, that is, take steps that help us gain a sense of mastery and enjoyment, it helps us connect with God and with other people, and we will find our feelings begin to change as well. It is easy for depressed people to tell themselves, "I can't do it" or "I don't feel like it."

If we desire to have self-control, we will do whatever it takes to get over depression. If we need to involve ourselves with other people, go to work, or help people in need, whatever it takes to make us feel worthwhile and significant, we will do it even if we don't feel like it. Feelings are deceptive, and emotions cannot be trusted to reveal the truth about our lives. Emotions are a part of our human nature and we shouldn't deny or suppress them, just control them. We can control our emotions, if we depend on the power of God. The apostle Paul said, "But we have this treasure in jars of clay to show that this all-surpassing power is from God and not from us. We are hard pressed on every side, but not crushed; perplexed, but not in despair; persecuted, but not abandoned; struck down, but not destroyed" (II Corinthians 4:7-9).

The Truth About Anger

What is anger? Many people try to ignore anger or try to make it a sinful emotion that God has condemned. Some people feel that we should never get angry and that if we can rid our life of anger, we will be a happy. The problem of anger in our lives cannot be dealt with so simply. Like taxes, anger doesn't just go away, even if we decide it ought to. The truth is that anger is not always bad. God is angry at times (Psalm 7:11; Exodus 4:14; Deuteronomy 29:27). Jesus experienced anger when he saw the hard hearts of the Pharisees and later when He cleansed the Temple (Mark 3:5; John 2:17).

The apostle Paul got angry many times and one time he got angry with the church at Corinth for not getting angry with the man who was living with his father's wife (I Corinthians 5). There were other times when the apostle got angry with individuals or churches but he always had their best interests at heart (Galatians 2:11-14; Acts 16:18; 17:16; II Corinthians 7:9-11). We do not see Paul getting angry in a vengeful way or with jealousy in his heart. Paul points out the fact that we need to engage in righteous anger and act accordingly when faced with sin in the church and the world.

The simple emotion of anger is not always harmful or unloving. It is what we do when we are angry that has moral significance. Next to love, anger is the most common emotion experienced in life. Many psychologists believe that anger is the primary emotion experienced by a person in depression.

It is easy in our culture to tell ourselves that we can't control angry feelings. There is a difference between being "angry" and "venting" anger. There is a difference in being "assertive" and being "violent" when expressing anger. "Venting" is basically a concept, held by some psychiatrists and psychologists, which asserts that our emotions are like a steam boiler, which must release pressure by releasing steam to avoid an explosion. I have never seen any research or experimental evidence to confirm this theory. In fact, this theory flies in the face of Scripture. The Bible tells us that we can release our emotions in an acceptable way.

In the book of James, we find a Scripture that encourages us to "be quick to listen, slow to speak and slow to become angry, for man's anger does not bring about the righteous life that God desires" (James 1:19, 20). In my experience, people who have been counseled to use objects or the therapist himself as a target for their venting, have been void of the desire to control their emotions. This process does not encourage "self-control." In fact, I believe it does just the opposite. It encourages a lack of self-control.

Whether it is an adult venting or a child throwing a temper tantrum, all venting should be discouraged. I believe that acceptance of "venting" in our society has caused us to experience a culture where "road rage" is common. Expressing our feelings with control and a caring attitude should be taught as proper behavior.

Anger is defined in most textbooks as, "an emotional response of the mind and body to a stimulus." Paul wrote, "In your anger do not sin: do not let the sun go down while you are still angry, and do not give the devil a foothold" (Ephesians 4:26, 27). He is telling us, by inspiration from God, to deal with the issue of anger before the day is over. How we deal with our anger is at the heart of the issue of "self-control."

Paul makes it plain that we can control our anger, and we had better control it or it will cause us to sin. Anger is an emotional response to a stimulus and when the stimulus is withdrawn, the anger responses will cease. That is, if we don't tell ourselves how unfair and unjust life is.

We need to learn to reject absolute statements and accept the truth, even if it causes us some pain and discomfort. Statements, such as, "I can't live without him/her" or "I can't stand it if I'm not liked by everyone" or "It would be terrible if he/she rejected me," should be erased from our minds. Such statements cause a lot of anxiety. Instead we should tell ourselves truth statements, such as, "I can stand it if I lose a loved one; it will be hard and painful, but I can make it."

The truth is not everyone will like us and it hurts to be rejected by people, but we can deal with it and get on with our lives. When we are rejected we must tell ourselves, "it is not the end of the world!" The Bible teaches us that growth and maturity come from pain and hardship (Hebrews 12:7-11; James 1:2-4).

The apostle Paul tells us, "Do not be anxious about anything, but in everything, by prayer and petition, with thanksgiving, present your requests to God, and the peace of God, which transcends all understanding, will guard your hearts and your minds in Christ Jesus" (Philippians 4:6, 7).

Paul is telling us that we need not be anxious about anything in this world, but have faith in a God who loves us and wants to give us peace. Most people in the world want peace and never find it because they look in all the wrong places and refuse to believe in the God who has the power to give us peace.

Filling Our Empty Places

When the apostle Paul stated (in a Roman prison) that he had learned to be content in whatever state he was in, he proclaimed a truth that many never experience in life (Philippians 4:11-13). Paul was saying that with God he could be content in any circumstance. In other words, it was not the circumstance that made him content or happy but the mindset he had and his relationship with God. It is not the circumstances in life that make us content, but our belief systems and our trust in God.

In the Gospel of Matthew, Jesus tells the story of a man who had an evil spirit (during the age when God allowed evil spirits to possess people) and it was cast out of him (Matthew 12:43-45). Then the man was (metaphorically) swept clean and what remained was an empty place. It is inferred that the man did not replace the evil spirit with the teachings of God's Spirit. Eventually the evil spirit came back in full force and found the place swept clean and empty. Jesus said of the evil spirit, "Then it goes and takes with it seven other spirits more wicked than itself, and they go in and live there." I believe the moral of this story is that we must sweep our lives clean of sin and continue to keep close to the Lord (James 4:6-10).

When we begin to become discontented with our circumstances, we have a tendency to fantasize about what we would like them to be. At this point, we begin a thought process that breaks down our inhibitions against sin and our mind starts to have sinful thoughts, which will ultimately lead to sinful actions (Matthew 5:21-30). Then comes the process of leaving the Lord behind and not letting Him have a distinct place in our lives.

When we rationalize to excuse our sinful thoughts and actions, we set ourselves up for being susceptible to temptation. Jesus said, "No one can serve two masters. Either he will hate the one and love the other or he will be devoted to the one and despise the other" (Matthew 6:24). Paul gives us the solution to sinful fantasies when he says, "We demolish arguments and every pretension that sets itself up against the knowledge of God, and we take captive every thought to make it obedient to Christ" (II Corinthians 10:5).

When we become discontented with our circumstances, we begin to think of ways to change them to feel better about ourselves and to find contentment. When this happens, we cease to rely on God to give us contentment and the acting out of sinful behavior is just around the corner (James 1:13-15). We have gotten off the track of trust in God to give us contentment and have begun to look to the world and its fleshly desires to find it. Paul was not equating contentment with complacency. Sometimes we can change our circumstances in a Godly way to make our life better, but we must not trust in our circumstances alone; if we do, we will fail.

When we were converted to Christ, we swept our lives clean of the sinful nature (Romans 6:1-7). If we don't continue in a prayerful relationship with God, a vacuum will begin to exist and Satan and the world will readily fill it with sinful thoughts, desires and behavior. It is vitally important that our thought processes and belief systems be
programmed with the truth that God has the power to give us peace and contentment in whatever state we are in (Philippians 4:4-13).

Paul is telling us that we really can have self-control when he says, "No temptation has seized you except what is common to man. And God is faithful; he will not let you be tempted beyond what you can bear. But when you are tempted, he will also provide a way out so that you can stand up under it" (I Corinthians 10:13). We must have faith in Him and trust in His word.

Many people in the world believe that happiness is by luck or circumstance and that we have very little or no control over it. Without a belief in and a relationship with the Lord, there is no reason to believe in the fact that we can have joy in this world without luck or favorable circumstances. I'm convinced that dysfunctional behavior is caused when a person believes, "circumstances determine happiness."

Living With a Perfectionist

Judy came to my office one day wanting help. Jason, her husband, was a perfectionist and it was destroying their marriage. Judy was distraught and ready to leave her husband. She told me Jason was controlling and he always criticized her, he was never satisfied with what she did at home. He expected her to not only wash his clothes but to press and starch his shirts and arrange all of his clothes in a certain order in their dresser and in their closet. He expected the kids to have all their toys in the toy box, except the ones they were playing with. The house had to be spotless at all times, and he inspected it every night when he got home. If it didn't meet his expectations, he would go into a long tirade and then not talk to her the rest of the night. Judy told me she was leaving Jason if he didn't get counseling. "I can't live this way any longer, I feel like a slave in my own house and I don't love him anymore," she told me. They had been married for eight years.

When Jason finally came into my office, I could see that he really didn't want to be there and he didn't comprehend that there was any problem in his marriage. "I don't see any reason why I have to be here; if it weren't for my wife threatening me, I wouldn't have come," he said. It is beyond me why some husbands don't see a problem in their marriage when their wives threaten to leave them.

Jason had a problem with perfectionism and unrealistic expectations. In his mind, he thought that he knew best how things should be and that everything should be in a certain order. If things weren't in the order he prescribed, it would mean that he failed as a husband and father. It became apparent after a few counseling sessions that Jason suffered from the lie, "Unless things are in a certain order and tidy, I cannot feel good about myself and find peace."

It was hard for Jason to see this lie in his life. He had been taught in his childhood to believe that "an orderly life is a happy life." His parents constantly berated and rejected him when he didn't do things the way they thought he should have. They had transferred their insecurities on to him and he was suffering for it.

Jason was also an "introvert," and it has been proven to me in my counseling practice that introverts have a temperamental tendency towards perfectionism. This, of course, doesn't mean he couldn't control his desires to be perfect, he just didn't believe that such behavior was wrong and harmful to his relationships. His mind was so programmed to believe the lie, "his way was the right way," that it took a long time for him to recognize it and remove it.

After several counseling sessions the removal process was completed. "This process of changing my belief systems is very frightening, I feel very insecure during this time," he said. It took Jason several months of practice to finally fight off the urge to arrange things or expect his wife to have the house a certain way. He was finally replacing his lies with the truth.

Jason found peace of mind through cognitive therapy and a growing faith in God to help him through the struggle of overcoming perfectionism. When we came to the final stages of the counseling process he said, "I have never felt more secure in my relationship with God and my family." I feel like a gigantic boulder has been taken off my shoulders and I am free again." Jesus said, "the truth will set you free" (John 8:32).

As human beings we have a tendency to reach into what I call our "Gratification Grab Bag." When we feel insecure about our lives, we reach into this bag and find the behavior that best suits us to make us feel better about ourselves. For the beautiful woman who is being ignored by her husband, it may be flirtation with another man. For the not so beautiful woman it might be to max out the credit cards, or if obese, she might go on an eating binge. For the man it might be sexual immorality, drinking, drugs or in Jason's case, perfectionism. Whatever the gratification is for the moment, it doesn't last long and the result is usually guilt or a feeling of disgust. Like an alcoholic after a night of drinking, the next day the pleasure is gone and the results are painful.

I believe that overeating, anorexia nervosa, bulimia, substance abuse and other self-indulgent behaviors are caused to one degree or another by the lies people tell themselves about the circumstances they live in. They fail when they want to change, because they engage in self-destructive behavior. Paul said it best when he said, "Everything is permissible for me, but not everything is beneficial. Everything is permissible for me, but I will not be mastered by anything" (I Corinthians 6:12).

God wants us to be free from the belief systems that enslave us. He wants us to understand that His will for our lives will free us and give us the joy we all want in life. The apostle John said, "This is the love of God: to obey his commands. And his commands are not burdensome" (I John 5:3).

The Peril Of Unrealistic Expectations

I do not have the right to be angry when another person does not live up to my expectations. There is no necessary connection between the behavior of another person and our anger. It doesn't matter how unfairly, unjustly or thoughtlessly someone has
behaved toward us, we are angry because of our own self-talk.

I do have a choice whether or not to be or remain angry. "Everyone should be QUICK to listen, SLOW to speak and SLOW to become angry" (James 1:19). Someone else cannot make me angry if I choose not to be. It is my choice, and I must take responsibility for it.

Too often we allow "unrealistic expectations" to set us up for a fall. They set us up for disappointment and heartbreak. It is not "dreadful" or even especially unusual if others do things I don't like or fail to treat me as well as I treat them. We waste a lot of time, energy and thought when we brood over the offenses of others. If I have expectations of my wife or my children or anybody in my world, I must evaluate whether or not they are realistic for that person to fulfill.

We are all different and many of us come from different backgrounds. To expect everybody in my world to do or be what I want them to be is impossible. Some people may not be able to perform exactly as I expect them to and they may have different belief systems than I have.

All of us have sinned, according to God's word (Romans 3:23). The people in your life will not always be kind, just, loving, and thoughtful to you. Learn to deal with it! None of us behave perfectly and fairly in every instance. We must learn to ACCEPT one another, with all of our quirks and idiosyncrasies, just as Christ has accepted us (Roman 15:7).

When we get caught up in the SHOULD'S and OUGHT TO'S, we set ourselves up for frustration. Judy continued to tell herself that Jason "ought to" be nice to her and not expect so much of her. She kept telling herself that he "should" treat her and the children right and not be so demanding. We could all sympathize with Judy, she was right and Jason was wrong. We could become indignant towards Jason and cry out that he shouldn't act that way because it's not Christ-like.

Vindictive anger towards someone who is unjust and cruel, is usually futile. Such people do not have the same mindset as we do and our "should's" and "ought to's" are not theirs and they usually have little effect on the controller or the perfectionist. All they do is cause us emotional pain and heartache. We can learn to accept people even when we don't condone their behavior.

The Agape Principle

The "Agape Principle" requires of us that we love our neighbor regardless of what he/she believes or how he/she behaves towards us (Matthew 19:19). "Agape" is the noun form of the Greek word for "unconditional" love. When Jesus said, "Love your neighbor as yourself," he used this word (agapao – verb form) in this passage when describing how we should love our neighbor. "Phileo" is the verb form in the Greek for "affectionate" love. "Phileo" is not normally used as a command to "love" someone. "Agapao" can be commanded because it is a type of love that doesn't require emotional attachment.

When speaking of how "agapao" is used in reference to God (I John 4:9, 10), W.E. Vine says, "But obviously this is not the love of complacency, or affection, that is, it was not drawn out by an excellency in its objects."[5] That's how Jesus could love us and command us to love and serve our enemies (Matthew 5:44-48; Romans 5:8; 12:17-21; 13:9).

I believe that a good biblical definition of "agape" love would be, "the kind of love that does not require affection, but does require that I do what is best for someone even if he/she doesn't like it or thinks that it is unloving." As a Christian, God expects me to love everyone unconditionally, whether I like them or not.

In the case of Jason's wife, she needed to learn how to "agape" love him in spite of his perfectionism. It is easy for us to blame Jason for his abusive and controlling behavior towards his wife, but she also has a responsibility to deal with it in a Christian manner. All marriages, where there is a controlling partner, certainly do not turn out this positive after counseling. When the mate, who is being controlled, tries to stop the controller by nagging, complaining or enabling, it usually fails and only makes things worse.

When I counsel women, who are married to men who are controllers (women can be controllers too), I teach them how to be "passively resistant."

They should not be rebellious towards their husbands, but they can learn how to not "react" to the manipulations of a controller. God ordained that the husband be the head (leader not dictator) of the wife, and that she should submit to his leadership, as he continues to honor and love her (Ephesians 5:22-33).

The concept of REACTING to the controller's manipulation is important here. To "react" is to "counteract" and it is a controlling action in and of itself. We usually "react" to people we know are trying to control us, but when we do, we actually feed into a power trip the insecure controller is on. He is looking for some kind of reaction that will reflect his/her power over the person he/she is trying to manipulate. No matter how negative the "reaction," the controller gains a sense of power by it. I realize that this comparison is a play on words, but please let me have the liberty to use words in a way that best describes the dynamic that is going on between the controller and the controllee. I will use the word "respond" as opposed to the word "react."

I teach my counselees to "respond" in a non-emotional way that does not reinforce the belief system of the controller that he has power over someone. The controllee must be careful that his/her body language does not reflect a reaction. I realize that this is hard to do and that we all have emotions that are hard to control at times. God can give us the power to accomplish it. I am not saying that the controllee should not get angry at times, but that the anger must be under control.

When a person refuses to enable a controller, it is not rebellion, but it is self-control. Such a response will usually have the effect of causing the controller to turn up the heat for a while, because he is not getting the results he thinks he needs to claim power and feel good about himself. This type of behavior (refusing to react to the controller) is sending the message to the controller that he needs to start taking responsibility for his actions. The goal is to change the belief system and replace it with the truth. The truth is, we don't need to control and manipulate people to feel better about ourselves. When we humble ourselves, God will exalt us (James 4:10).

The Blame Game

Many people in our world are eager and willing to blame anything and everything but themselves for their behavior. We live in a very litigious society where people are quick to sue anyone for the slightest reasons, and because our courts cater to them, people are not held responsible for their sins (or as some would rather put it, "their mistakes").

We have a great capacity to "shift the blame" in our society. This propensity goes way back to our original parents. When confronted by God regarding the violation of God's only prohibition in the Garden of Eden, Eve could only say that, "the devil made me do it" (paraphrased). And Adam was no better when he shifted the blame on Eve and God as well (Genesis 3:12, 13). Nothing much has changed since then.

Modern humanistic psychology has been obsessed with the idea that man is not responsible for his conduct. You see it everywhere, on TV and radio talk shows, in the media and in our institutions of higher learning.

"In a fascinating book entitled, ' Nation of Victims,'subtitled, 'The Decay of the American Character, Charles Sykes argues that there has been a 'fundamental transformation of American cultural values and notions of character and personal responsibility.' In example after example, the author shows that 'American life is
increasingly characterized by the plain insistence, I am a victim; I am not responsible; it's not my fault.'"[6]

God does not allow us to blame others when we sin or fail to do what is right. He doesn't allow us to do so even when we make minor mistakes. If you find yourself having received too much change at a grocery store after counting it, do you go back to the checker and explain the mistake and give him back the difference? When we come to these kinds of decisions, we must take the responsibility to do what is right and true. We must live the life of truth and responsibility, always seeking the good of all men and modeling the righteousness of Christ (I Peter 1:13-16).

Christian Moral Standards

A value is that which is esteemed, prized, or deemed worthwhile and desirable by a person or culture. Christian values stem from faith in Christ Jesus and the message he taught. Christian faith causes us to look upon certain ways of thinking, acting, and living as worthwhile and desirable; these special ways of thinking, acting, and living constitute a system of Christian values.

An example of a Christian value is respect for human dignity of each person with whom we come in contact, which stems from the commandment Jesus Christ gave us to love our neighbor as ourselves. This Christian value determines how we think, feel, and act in regard to other people, races, and nations. Even though we may not like these people and even, at times, consider them enemies.

We prize all other human beings because of their dignity as creatures of God and because we all were created by Him. This respect and love for others is closely linked to the commandment to "love God with all your heart, with all our soul and with all your mind and your neighbor as yourself" (Matthew 22:37).

The Sin Factor

The Christian counselor needs to make a deep and radical diagnosis of the average cause of self-control problems and disorders and that is: "sin is the root of all of mankind's lack of self-control and the problems that accompany it." When Paul says, "All things are lawful for me, but not all things are profitable. All things are lawful for me, but I will not be mastered by anything," he is saying that our own sinful desires create the problem, not the temptation itself (I Corinthians 6:12; James 1:13-15 NASB).

Christian counselors today have sometimes been led astray by secular psychology, which often removes responsibility for a condition from the shoulders of the counselee. They readily attribute counselee difficulties to some past trauma or series of traumas visited upon the counselee by others, or to hurt feelings caused by the sins of others, or to powerlessness brought on by the helpless victimizing of the counselee by demonic forces. One of the duties of the Christian counselor is to teach counselees how to repent. Repentance means, literally, "being sorry for my actions and thoughts and changing the way I live and think."

The apostle Paul rebuked the church at Corinth for allowing a member there to live in adultery. Paul commended them later for acting on the command to disfellowship this adulterer and rejoiced that they had experienced a "godly repentance" as opposed to a "worldly repentance" (I Corinthians 5; II Corinthians 7:8-11).

A worldly repentance is a repentance that says, "I'm sorry, because I got caught." A godly repentance says, "I'm sorry for what I did; I understand the evilness of it; I deeply regret it and will seek never to do that again" (James 4:6-10).

The concept of repentance is not just experiencing mournful feelings about your sins, even though you will begin to feel bad about them when you notice their effect on God, on your relationship with others, and on yourself. It isn't just feeling sorrowful that is at the heart of repentance, it is literally "changing the mind" (Romans 12:2). It is developing a new mind that is willing to submit to the will of God and His Spirit (Ephesians 4:20-24; Romans 8:6-11).

Review Questions

1. What is the cause of depression as described in this book?
2. What is the truth about anger?
3. What is the significance of "filling our empty places?"
4. What is the purpose of the "Gratification Grab Bag?"
5. Why do people blame others or other things for their sins and mistakes?
6. How would you describe the concept of "reacting?"
7. How would you describe the concept of "unrealistic expectations?"
8. Why does a "perfectionist" have a strong tendency to be a "controller?"

Chapter Four

DEALING WITH ANGER ISSUES

The apostle Paul tells us to deal with our anger within the time frame of a twenty-four hour day when he says, "do not let the sun go down while you are still angry!" This means that we must deal with it before the sun goes down. If we do not, it will begin to tempt us to sin (Ephesians 4:26, 27). From these two verses we can see the moral distinction between GOOD anger and BAD anger. "Good anger" is when you control it and "bad anger" is when it controls you.

I don't believe in the "anger management" concept of therapy that is proposed by so many counselors and psychologists in workshops and seminars today. This method usually requires you to manage anger in a way that involves venting or something similar to it. I believe the Bible teaches us to DEAL with anger in a responsible way. This requires expression of feelings in a loving manner and it requires taking responsibility for those feelings.

When we deal with anger issues, we must not blame others or our circumstances. Dealing with anger means that we speak the truth in love and communicate our feelings and take responsibility for our feelings and actions. It's okay to be angry, just take responsibility for choosing to be.

Paul also tells us that if we don't deal with our anger before the end of the day, the devil will have an advantage over us, in our emotional state, to tempt us to sin. This means that we cannot allow ourselves to be in denial or avoidance when it comes to recognizing our anger. When we are in denial or avoidance, we may feel relieved that the problem isn't before us for the moment, but it will pop up again somehow. The human psyche has a way of revealing anger issues (we have been denying or avoiding) in sometimes mysterious and self-destructive ways.

"A growing amount of evidence suggests that suppressed anger does relate to hypertension and heart disease. Hypertensives, who are quick to respond physiologically to stress, show high amounts of suppressed anger. Findings also confirm a link between aggressive behaviors and painful muscle tension."[7]

Dr. Armand Nicholi II, a psychiatrist at Massachusetts General Hospital and on the teaching staff of Harvard Medical School, stated, "A person cannot get sick without a stress factor being involved. Buried emotions of anger and fear are the most important stress factors in physical illness."[8]

Dr. Robert Good was asked, "Why did cancer take so many and, yet, not take others of the same environment, such as identical twins?" He said that, "it is the presence of emotional stressors, particularly unresolved anger. The hormones that the body releases under prolonged stress, including the hormone adrenaline, inhibit the body's normal ability to fight and destroy cancer cells."[9]

Much of the research done on prolonged anger or stress shows that it produces many health risks and can ultimately produce premature death. We must learn to express anger in a biblical way so that we can maintain better physical and emotional health.

Anger is a Defense Mechanism

When I first heard this story a few years ago, I couldn't believe it, but I am told that the following is a true story:

"A couple in Switzerland began to fight in a way that brought a battle of mayhem. It all began when the husband canceled one vacation trip too many for his wife. She expressed her disappointment by pouring bicarbonate of soda into the fish tank, wiping out his rare tropical fish. A long argument followed, then he grabbed a selection of his wife's diamond jewelry and threw it into the garbage disposal. She responded by flinging all his stereo equipment into the swimming pool. He then doused her $200,000 wardrobe – fur coats, designer gowns and all – with liquid bleach."

Then things began to go downhill. "She poured a gallon of paint all over his $70,000 Ferrari. So he kicked a hole in the $180,000 Picasso original she loved. She had just opened the seacocks of his 38-foot yacht, causing it to sink at its dock, when the couple's daughter came home and saw what had been going on. She called the police. They were powerless to do anything. It was not illegal for the couple to destroy their own property. Eventually the family lawyer managed to arrange a truce."[10]

As ironic and silly as this story may seem, many people live in homes where vengeful emotions are out of hand and anger rules the day and people lose control of their senses.

Understanding Our Thinking-Feeling Process

A = Activating Event

B = Belief System

C = Consequence (behavior or feeling)

How We Usually Regard What Happens
A ──────▶ C

What Actually Happens
A ──────▶ B ──────▶ C

Irrational Beliefs That Produce Anger

1. I must be loved by every person I believe to be significant and important.
2. I must control attitudes and affections of others.
3. I must have a high degree of order and certainty to be happy.
4. I must be competent and successful in all things I attempt.
5. I must be treated well by other people or I will be emotionally disturbed.
6. I must have no bad experiences in my past or the past will continually ruin my future and never really be overcome.
7. I must have a life that is entirely pleasant, without any frustration, discomfort or pain or life will be unbearable.
8. I must make everybody happy and content.
9. I believe unhappiness is caused by my circumstances.
10. I must have all my needs met.

These lies create perceived threats and angry emotions that can cause us to engage in self-destructive behavior. The following are options that can help us deal with anger:

Options for Dealing with Anger

1. CONFIRM IT! (Evaluate whether or not it is worth responding to)
2. POSTPONE IT! (Evaluate how, when, and where to express it)
3. EXPRESS IT! (Expressing it in "I messages," not venting)

    a. "I messages" require that we be:
       1) Non-accusative in our speech
       2) Willing to describe our feelings
       3) Willing to take responsibility for our feelings

An example of someone using an accusative message would be: "You don't love me because you didn't …!" An example of a non-accusative "I message" would be: "I felt hurt and angry when you didn't …!" Speaking the truth in love (Ephesians 4:15).

When we choose to "postpone" for a day or two, we are dealing with our anger, if we have a plan to deal with it and we execute it. "I messages" reduce defensive responses.

Anger is a "defense mechanism." It is a natural response of the mind and body when threatened. God has given our bodies the hormone "adrenaline" to prepare us for physical threats. He has also built into our emotional makeup the ability to get angry as a way of preparing our minds against a psychological threat.

Anger is a natural response for the defense and preservation of important belief systems and physical health. It is a response with the intent of preserving:

- PERSONAL WORTH
- ESSENTIAL NEEDS
- BASIC CONVICTIONS

When our self-esteem is threatened, we tend to be defensive and angry. When our essential needs, such as emotional needs and physical needs are threatened, we get angry and develop a defensive posture. And when we feel that our basic convictions on vital subjects are under attack, we become defensive. In my counseling practice I have observed the following progressive steps in the lives of troubled people:

Five Steps to an Emotional Crisis

1. PERCEIVED THREATS (threats that are either real or imaginary)
2. FEAR/ANXIETY (fear and anxiety immediately follow)
3. ANGER/BITTERNESS (anger, unchecked, turns to bitterness)
4. DISCOURAGEMENT/HOPELESSNESS (follows failure to resolve)
5. RESIGNATION/DEPRESSION (which can lead to clinical depression)

Psychologically, the above steps will be experienced sequentially even if not consciously, but they can be controlled. Again, the Bible says that we must deal with our anger before the day ends. Once we have realized our anger, it should be a RED FLAG for us to recognize that there is a PERCEIVED THREAT that we must deal with. It should alert us to a threat that is either real or imaginary.

A "real threat" is recognized by the immediate potential harm we perceive in our presence. An "imaginary threat" is one in which we perceive a threat to our being, but there is no immediate danger. It could be imaginary in the sense of a supposed attack on our self-worth, or on our basic belief systems, even though there seems to be no immediate danger.

I am convinced that all "anger responses" are responses to perceived threats. In other words, every time we feel angry there is a perceived threat in our belief systems. If it is real, then we need to deal with it as best we can. If it is not, then we must examine our thoughts and make sure that we are telling ourselves the truth. Anger can become a programmed response (a defense mechanism) to a perceived threat.

I also believe that the "dysfunctional family" is a model of angry responses to perceived threats. It is a model of false belief systems and how they create in the "family system" a survival mentality that adversely affects the whole family. It affects their interpersonal relationships and creates an inability on the part of the family members to communicate their feelings and to develop problem-solving skills.

Anger and fear are emotions that rule the hearts of dysfunctional family members every day. The primary criteria that qualify families as dysfunctional are: a lack of personal identity of individual members, a lack of communication skills and a lack of problem-solving skills to deal with everyday problems that arise in interpersonal relationships.

The Dysfunctional Family

The systems model in family therapy assumes that the "nuclear family" is the basic context in which problems occur. The family is seen as a rule-governed organism that has a dynamic, which transcends that of its separate participants. If it is our intention to really understand a particular individual, it is argued, then we must become thoroughly familiar with his or her family system. "A 'system' can be defined as a group of interconnected or interrelated parts, which mutually interact across time."[11] Systems have distinct characteristics and are made up of their parts and the relationships of their parts, and thus the system is greater than the sum of its individual parts.

Systems are characterized by an "interdependency," which includes how the parts influence each other. There are no insignificant parts. Systems have boundaries that differentiate one system from another system. A system is an organism.

A particular member's dysfunctional behavior, under the systems theory, reflects a family system that is dysfunctional. The "troubled member" reveals a family in trouble. If a family is dysfunctional, the family relationships that support the lack of stability must be dealt with, or long-term change in the troubled member is unlikely. Since the dysfunctional family is a "closed" system, it makes sense to explore how each family member affects and influences the other.

Co-dependency Issues

Originally the word "co-dependence" was limited to the study of alcoholic families. It was first used to label the spouse of the alcoholic. Later, as "family systems thinking" came to be used, the "whole" family was seen as co-dependent. Co-dependency is the most common symptom of a dysfunctional family.

In every dysfunctional family there is a "primary stressor" and each family member adapts to this stress in an attempt to control and appease the stressor. Each member then becomes involved in adapting to the stressor as long as the stress exists. Each becomes co-dependent on the stressor.

This state of readiness was intended by nature to be a survival state. In dysfunctional families, it is often the normal state. When a threat actually occurs, the person responds with "survival behaviors." Such behaviors include denial, dissociation, repression or withdrawal and anger.

Survival behaviors are actual responses to the violent (and sometimes passive manipulations) and threatening behavior of the primary stressor. The adult child of a dysfunctional family learns to survive by developing certain patterns of behavior. As the child of a dysfunctional family grows up, these survival behaviors continue even though they are now disconnected from the original stressor. These survival behaviors feel normal since they are the patterns one used every day of his/her early life in order to survive.

As an adult, survival behaviors are unnecessary and can be very unhealthy. While they were once protective, now they are destructive. There must be a change in belief systems for the member to change his/her behavior.

Survival behaviors are hard to give up. They have become very familiar. They helped the person survive by developing a kind of power that resulted from sacrificing self. In every case the person threatened develops a dependency on things outside himself to the point of self-neglect. In the counseling cases I have been involved with there has always been an underlying sense of anger and bitterness.

I believe that anger is a defense mechanism for the dysfunctional member who possesses a "victim mentality" in most situations in life. He/she is always lacking in fulfilling their essential needs and they do not become self-actualized. A dysfunctional family member believes that his identity lies outside himself in a substance, activity or another person. He has sold himself and he is not able to be his own person. The person then develops a "survival belief system," which produces the following programmed responses: people-pleasing, self-debasing, anti-social behavior, denial, distrust of others, intimidating and controlling, blaming, avenging, habitual lying, manipulation, unhealthy expression of anger, avoidance or rejection of feelings, lack of relational and problem-solving skills.

Co-dependent children have given up their own identity in order to take care of their parent(s) or the needs of the family system. The co-dependent must live a life of survival, like animals, always on guard against threats from the outside. Thus the continuing, underlying emotion of anger is always under the surface ready to explode. Many times co-dependents try to make themselves indispensable by taking care of others. They are willing to do whatever it takes to be loved or feel significant.

Once a person believes that his identity lies outside himself in a substance, activity or another person, he has sold himself and he is not able to fulfill his own essential needs. He/she is not able to truly love and be loved as long as he/she believes that they are not worthy of love and must always be on the alert to please others.

God created in us basic needs. We need to be: loved, respected, needed, capable, significant, and secure in our self-worth (Romans 12:9-18). Neglecting such essential needs, to serve others (especially the primary stressor in the family), is not healthy spiritually, emotionally or psychologically. God wants us to serve others and put their needs first, but not at the expense of our self-worth, or as a response to a threat. Our service to others should be an act of the will (Philippians 2:3, 4)!

The Principle of Boundaries

In their very popular book, "Boundaries," Drs. Cloud and Townsend state that the purpose of boundaries is not to put limits on others, but to put limits on ourselves and our exposure to others, who may be using or manipulating us. In other words, boundaries are limits on how we allow others to influence us and are vital to our own emotional, psychological and spiritual health.

This problem is usually seen in the context of the controller vs. the compliant person. When the controller seeks to control others by manipulation or intimidation, it is sinful and harmful to a relationship. The Bible tells us that we must be responsible for our feelings and our actions.

In Paul's letter to the churches of Galatia, he says that we should, "Carry each other's burdens, and in this way you will fulfill the law of Christ." In another verse Paul says, "For each one should carry his own load" (Galatians 6:2, 5). These two verses seem contradictory at first glance until you examine the Greek words and their definitions.

The Greek word for "burden" in verse two is "baros" meaning, "a weight, anything pressing on one physically."[12] It could be equated to a giant boulder that is too much for one man to carry. The Greek word for "load" in verse five is "phortion." Vine says, "The difference between 'phortion' and 'baros' is, that 'phortion' is simply something to be borne, without reference to its weight, but 'baros' always suggests what is heavy or burdensome."[13] It could be said that "baros" represents a boulder of immense weight and "phortion" represents something as light as a "backpack" for hiking.

What God is really telling us, through the apostle Paul, is that we are to help those who can't carry the load because it is too much for them, but we should take responsibility for our own burdens that we are capable of carrying.

If we are not willing to take on our own responsibilities when we are capable, we are sinning before God. When we "enable" others by carrying their load when they are capable, we are enabling them to be irresponsible and are therefore sinning against the will of God.

I believe the above statements with all my heart, and I believe that we must be strong and set limits on others in regards to their influence on us when they use us to fulfill their responsibilities. When we allow them to be irresponsible, we encourage their lack of commitment to God and their slothfulness in life (Matthew 25:26).

I think we can see how this principle applies to parenting. When people learn to be responsible, accept their own identity, and depend on God for their happiness rather than circumstances, they will learn to control their anger.

Letting Go of Your Anger

Of the choices involving anger the most difficult one is to let it go. There are times when you may have appropriate convictions to communicate to others, yet assertiveness may not work. Or it could be that you have succeeded in making as many adjustments as possible in your world, yet imperfections continue to haunt you. At this point one of your options is to choose to let it go.

At times, your counselees may have no need to talk about their angry feelings toward others because they may be able to talk it over with the Lord and repent if necessary and then let it go. We as counselors do not need to try to force our counselees to confront someone they are angry with if it can be taken to the Lord and best be handled that way. Learning to let go of our anger is sometimes a reflection of "walking by faith, not by sight" (II Corinthians 5:7).

Another problem is that a Christian brother or sister may have sinned against your counselee or he/she may have sinned against a brother or sister in the Lord. This is when the Christian who has such a problem with another Christian should go to that person and work it out in a biblical sense as instructed by our Lord Jesus (Matthew 18:15-18).

We are always responsible for our anger and the behavior that arises from it. It is not right to blame someone else and expect others to make right what we have wrongly created.

Review Questions

1. How would you describe anger as a "defense mechanism?"
2. What is the difference between "good" anger and "bad" anger?
3. What are the three options for dealing with anger?
4. What is the advantage in communicating in "I messages?"
5. How would you define the term "co-dependency?"
6. Why are they called "survival behaviors?"
7. How would you describe a "functional" home?
8. How would you define "boundaries" as used in this chapter?

Chapter Five

CREATING A POSITIVE SELF-WORTH

Is a consideration of self-esteem important? Some people think we are too self-centered anyway. God created in us the ability to instinctively learn in certain areas of our lives, such as: talking, eating, walking and developing a self-concept either negative or positive. God does not want us to think too highly or too lowly of ourselves. The apostle Paul said, "For by the grace given me I say to every one of you: Do not think of yourself more highly than you ought, but rather think of yourself with sober judgment, in accordance with the measure of faith God has given you" (Romans 12:3).

If we think too highly of ourselves, we become arrogant and prideful and believe we don't need God (James 4:6). If we think too lowly of ourselves, we become incompetent and ineffective for God, because then we don't believe He can love us, care for us or that we are capable of success (I Peter 5:7).

If we can't see that God loves us, then we can't do all things through Him (Philippians 4:13). We will not have the willpower or the faith to be effective and consistent in serving Him. We must believe that He is God and that He will reward those who diligently seek Him (Hebrews 11:6).

The Cause of Low Self-Worth

In most cases we are products of our own thinking, which was to a great degree conditioned by our environment when we were children. Our parents and significant others in our lives helped shape our self-concept by what they told us about our self-worth and how they treated us. We then became "conditioned" over a period of time by our negative interpretation of what others said about us.

When our self-talk becomes negative and repeated often, our minds believed these things to be true. When our belief systems are full of lies about our self-worth, we will act that way.

When we tell ourselves that we must please people to be liked or loved, we set ourselves up for disappointment. People eventually lose respect for people-pleasers. When we feel like our opinions don't matter, or other opinions are more important than ours, we allow others to manipulate and use us.

God wants us to love others as we "love ourselves" (Matthew 19:19). When Jesus said this, it seems that He assumed that the normal attitude of an emotionally healthy person is that he loves himself. God is the most powerful source we can draw from to develop a positive self-worth (John 3:16).

The Power of a Father's Influence

Carol was well dressed and had the appearance of an accomplished woman when she came to me for counseling. She was a very successful woman and had graduated from college with honors. She could not accept her accomplishments. She was also clinically depressed. "I don't feel good about myself," she said. "I want to sleep all the time; I don't want to go to work and I am not taking care of the children and the house like I should," she blurted out in my office. I advised her to make an appointment with a psychiatrist and get some medical help with her depression.

A doctor diagnosed her condition and prescribed an antidepressant. It took about ten days for the antidepressant to take affect so she could relax to the point where I could counsel her. As a Christian, Carol couldn't find any acceptance from God in her life. She felt that she had greatly disappointed Him and was a terrible sinner.

When I probed into her past, I didn't find any evidence of a terrible sin or a sordid and rebellious lifestyle. I did find evidence of a very demanding father, who never seemed to accept Carol on her own merits. He was very critical and constantly yelled at her. In her mind, he was very strict and didn't love her. She believed that she was a failure at anything she did because she couldn't please him.

Carol married a man who was very much like her father. In my counseling ministry I have found that roughly ninety percent of the women I counsel, who have very demanding fathers (accepting their daughters only on the basis of performance), marry men just like them. They finally give up trying to please their fathers, because they conclude it is impossible. They subconsciously select men as husbands, who are like their fathers, hoping to create a relationship of love and acceptance to feel fulfilled.

The fascinating aspect of this is that these women have a tendency to "transfer" feelings and fears they have for their fathers to God Himself. They tend to see God as very strict and demanding. They see Him as rejecting them because they couldn't meet His expectations. They see Him as unloving and unforgiving of them. There is no hope in their lives for love and acceptance, so they become depressed and sometimes suicidal.

I shared with Carol the fact that she viewed God just like she did her father. She had to learn that she had programmed her mind to think that God had rejected her just like her father did. I had to prove to her that God loves her and won't reject her.

The Road to a Positive Self-worth

The following are biblical steps to a positive concept of our self-worth:

- Claim a THEOLOGY of God – get to know God (James 4:8).
- Claim a healthy FELLOWSHIP – help build a healthy fellowship with other people (Hebrews 10:24, 25).
- Develop a healthy SELF-UNDERSTANDING. Realize your weaknesses and put them in the proper perspective (Galatians 6:1-5).
- Achieve a realistic SELF-DISCLOSURE and evaluation. Learn from your failures and seek help to overcome them (James 5:16).
- Set SPIRITUAL priorities and goals. Seek to be spiritual in your thinking rather than worldly. Create a daily prayer life (I Thessalonians 5:16-18).
- Learn new SKILLS and improve old ones (I Peter 4:10).
- Master CREATIVE talk. Learn to talk in spiritual terms and reject coarse joking and obscene language (Ephesians 5:3-5).
- Avoid SELF-DESTRUCTIVE influences. Find the "encouragers" and avoid the "discouragers" (Ephesians 4:29).

The Bible teaches the following truths about how God sees us:

- I will not DIMINISH myself – I am a creation of God (I John 4:19).
- I will not COMPARE myself negatively with others (Galatians 6:4).

- I will not engage in negative, destructive THINKING (Philippians 4:8).
- I accept my FAILURES and will learn from them (Romans 8:28).
- I accept God's FORGIVENESS when I repent (I John 1:7-10).
- I forgive myself, and I am FREE of the past (II Corinthians 5:17).
- I will now enjoy the PEACE that God promises me (Philippians 4:6, 7).
- I love myself for who I am and who I can be in CHRIST (Romans 5:8).

Low Self-Worth and Deviant Behavior

Most researchers have come to the conclusion that deviant behavior is caused by a person's environment, not his/her genetics. To this date there has been no reliable research that proves beyond a reasonable doubt that there is a genetic propensity towards violence, pedophilia, homosexuality or any other type of deviant behavior. I realize that in our society homosexuality has become generally accepted and defended, but the Bible says that it is sinful and deviant (Leviticus 18:22; Romans 1:21-27; I Corinthians 6:9).

Those who believe in God, as the author of the Bible, cannot fathom a God who would condemn a behavior that was genetically motivated and couldn't be helped. "Of the multi scores of studies that have searched for biological factors, the only ones done so far that indicate a biological cause have implicated abnormal hypothalamus development and hormonal imbalance."[14]

People are not born with a homosexual orientation; it is a result of choice. A distinction must be made between a homosexual "orientation" and homosexual "behavior." Someone with a "homosexual orientation" can change his/her orientation through biblical counseling.

The apostle Paul made it quite clear that such a change was possible when he said, "Do you not know that the wicked will not inherit the kingdom of God? Do not be deceived: Neither the sexually immoral nor idolaters nor adulterers nor male prostitutes nor homosexual offenders nor thieves nor the greedy nor drunkards nor slanderers nor swindlers, will inherit the kingdom of God. And that is what some of you were. But you were washed, you were sanctified, you were justified in the name of the Lord Jesus Christ and by the Spirit of our God" (I Corinthians 6:9-11). A "homosexual orientation" is simply a programmed way of thinking of the same sex being more attractive and desirable than the opposite sex.

When someone does not engage in homosexual activity (who has a homosexual orientation), it is possible for God to accept him/her, but he/she should have counseling to change his/her mindset and alleviate the constant temptation such an orientation causes.

There is no credible evidence of a genetic causation of this sexual orientation. It is a result of environment and a programming of belief systems. It is a choice someone makes in regard to his/her sexuality conditioned by cultural and environmental factors. "Sometimes nature is imperfect – chromosomes basically control sexual orientation and sometimes the gender distinction is not exact – nature deviates from the norm. Such a case does not make a person homosexual."[15] Dr. Paul Meier states, "All humans have both male and female sex hormones, and accordingly, homosexuality might be more of a temptation physiologically for those people who have nearly an even balance of these hormones."[16]

My research and personal counseling experience have proven to me that there are three types of marriage relationships: (1) The "Father-Dominant" is an emotionally and psychologically, unhealthy relationship. The father is harsh, autocratic and lacks relational skills. The wife is warm, compliant, fearful, frustrated and lonely. The children usually lack relational and communication skills, and have a strong tendency towards violence.

(2) The "Mother-Dominant" is also emotionally and psychologically unhealthy. In this relationship, the mother is controlling and dominant. Her husband is usually very nice, kind, passionate, compliant (usually incompetent at home and often at work) and is resentful of his wife. Men in this kind of relationship can have a tendency towards pedophilia, since they feel threatened by adult women, but they see children as non-threatening and accepting. The daughter is usually lacking in understanding of her feminine role, and the son, as well, lacks an understanding of his masculine role. This environment also distorts a child's understanding of sexual (homosexual vs. heterosexual) and leadership roles. "Boys become effeminate when they grow up identifying with their mothers instead of with their fathers."[17]

(3) The "Father-Led Home" is an emotionally, psychologically and spiritually healthy environment. The father in this relationship knows how to lead and discipline without dominating, nurture without spoiling, and be

vulnerable but firm. Providing a masculine role model of love and support that helps both the son and daughter (and his wife) understand their individual roles in marriage (Proverbs 22:6; I Peter 3:7).

Research also shows that nurturing fathers are vitally important in raising children, developing a healthy self-worth and an avoidance of deviant behavior. Several aspects are involved in the nurturant dimension of fathering. It is important for parents to show "affection" and "intimacy" to one another in spontaneous, non-self-conscious ways. "You have seen the sign that said, 'The greatest thing I can do for my children is to love their mother.' That's basic – that the father and mother love each other. And they need to love each other in ways that the children can see. That love between parents provides the backdrop for the love that the child experiences."[18]

Parents need to show such intimacy towards their children the same way. Fathers are especially important in the nurturing of their children. It is expected that mothers will nurture their children, but fathers (in this culture in the past) have not been motivated to nurture their children as a general rule. The modern day father is becoming more aware and motivated to do so.

"Current research in child development shows that the relationships children have with their fathers is very important in the personality development of their children. How do boys develop a sense of masculine identity and girls a sense of feminine identity? For many years child development studies have consistently highlighted the importance of fathers as role models."[19]
"These studies show that for fathers to be effective as masculine role models for their sons, they must be perceived as 'nurturant.'"[20] A "nurturing parent" is one who cares for, loves, accepts and properly disciplines his/her child. "Kindergarten boys' development of a masculine orientation was facilitated by warm, rewarding, nurturant fathers who openly expressed interest in their son's development of masculine traits."[21]

The understanding, expressive, and supportive responsiveness of nurturant fathers with their daughters has also been shown to be important in helping the daughters develop a feminine sex-role orientation. "Girls learn to appreciate and develop their femininity through their relationship with confident, caring and expressive fathers."[22]

An analysis of different parenting styles made the following summary: "Children whose parents were above average in 'warmth' tend to be securely attached to their parents and were more competent. These children also had high self-esteem, did well in school, and accepted limits on their behavior.

They were more considerate of other children and referred to internalized moral standards."[23]

Numerous studies show that children and adolescents who report strong parental support through "praise and communication, and expressing affection," scored high on measures of self-esteem. "An extensive analysis of the literature on parental support shows that the greater the parental support the less anti-social aggression in children, the less behavior problems in children, and the less drug abuse in children's behavior. In those studies, parental support was described as parenting behavior that was praising, approving, encouraging, helping, cooperating, and expressed in terms of endearment and physical affection."[24]

All of this research simply reinforces the truth already found in Scripture. "Fathers, do not exasperate your children; instead, bring them up in the training (KJV says "nurture") and instruction of the Lord" (Ephesians 6:4).

Good Parenting, the Secret to a Healthy Self-worth

Discipline is a God ordained responsibility of parents (Exodus 20:12; Deuteronomy 21:18-21; Colossians 3:20, 21). God does not condone child abuse or child beating. But He does condone corporal punishment with restraint. The proper balance of love, acceptance and discipline is absolutely vital to a child's positive self-worth. There are three important ways to show acceptance:

- Unconditional love (Romans 5:8; 15:7).
- Healthy communication (Ephesians 4:29; James 5:16).
- Appropriate discipline (Hebrews 12:5-11; Ephesians 6:4).

Acceptance of the child, no matter what he/she does, is vitally important for the child to feel loved and secure in his/her identity. It helps develop trust and self-worth in the child. This is how God parented King David. David committed a terrible sin when he committed adultery with Bathsheba and had her husband killed when she became pregnant. But God still accepted and loved David and when the time was right David repented. The love of God motivated him (II Samuel 11&12; Acts 13:22).

Parents sometimes think that "acceptance" is the same as "condoning." It is not the same, because acceptance means that the parent "agape loves" the child. It is an unconditional love that does not have to condone the sins of the child. Parents adversely affect a child's behavior by:

- Lack of parental affirmation and acceptance of the child.
- Being over-protective and not requiring child responsibility.
- Lack of attention to a child or parental favoritism of a child.
- Lack of parental firmness, or too much permissiveness.
- Lack of providing security and boundaries for the child.
- Lack of credibility because of parental inconsistency or dishonesty.
- Inappropriate child/parent relationships that distort proper roles.

There can be no effective discipline without some suffering or pain (Hebrews 12:7-11). Children need to know the consequences of violating the laws of man and nature. This helps them to grow up and be responsible. This does not mean that a parent has the right to physically, emotionally, sexually, or verbally abuse a child.

The following five rules are important in disciplining a child:

- Be willing, as parents, to agree on the forms of discipline you use.
- Be consistent with the forms of discipline you agreed upon.
- Be willing to accept the child while not condoning the behavior.
- Be sure that expectations of the child are understood and realistic.
- Be sure the discipline shapes the will without damaging the spirit.

Discipline must be coupled with love. Dr. Jack Raskin, Child Psychologist at Children's Orthopedic Hospital at the University of Washington in Seattle states, "The key to a healthy personality development lies in the child's close unbroken attachment in its early months to the people who care for him. If you give your children consistent love and discipline until the age of six, you'll find most of your work is done."

God tells parents to not withhold discipline from a child and that, "He who spares the rod hates his son." He also says, "Folly is bound up in the heart of a child; but the rod of discipline will drive it far from him," and "The rod of correction imparts wisdom, but a child left to himself disgraces his mother" (Proverbs 23:13, 14; 13:24; 22:15; 29:15).

Non-abusive spanking is most effective when:

- It is administered as a "last resort."
- It is administered with self-control.
- It is reserved for willful acts of defiance.
- It is administered in private (but not on the face).
- It is always followed by love and acceptance.

Social scientists tell us that spanking at the adolescent stage of the child attacks the self-esteem only, it does very little to discipline them. I believe it is better to set boundaries and restrict privileges as appropriate discipline when they begin to reach this stage. The modern culture, supported by misguided and permissive psychologists, has condemned "spanking" as physical abuse that engenders violence in the child. I have seen no research to prove such conclusions. It is evident that actual physical, emotional, and sexual abuse can and often does engender violence in a child, but God ordained corporal punishment, with appropriate restraint, does not fall into that category.

Responsible psychologists and psychiatrists encourage us to use proper discipline and be responsible as parents and know our boundaries. James Dobson states, "Yelling and nagging at children can become a habit, and an ineffectual one at that. It is like trying to steer a car by honking a horn. The parent must recognize that the most successful techniques of control are those that involve withholding something of importance to the child, but not something that is vital to his/her well-being. When you are defiantly challenged, win decisively. When the child asks, 'Who's in charge?' – tell him! When he mutters, 'Who loves me?' Take him in your arms and surround him with affection."[25]

God has allowed us to be stewards of our precious children; therefore, we do not "own" them (I Corinthians 4:2)! Remember that the purpose of discipline is to develop character and the purpose of parenting is to show the child guidance, acceptance and love. This is what the child needs and no one else on this earth can give it to him better than loving, responsible parents!

The Culture and Self-Worth

We often measure our self-worth by what our culture tells us. This usually causes us to think less of ourselves and low self-esteem is the result. The problem is that unfortunately, we also measure others by these values, usually to their loss of self-esteem. A vicious cycle continues; our children are measured by these values, compare themselves by these values, and, in turn, measure friends, siblings, and parents by these values (Galatians 6:4). Some of us win in this process, but many of us lose also. This cycle then repeats itself in following generations unless those people learn to incorporate new values.

Self-worth is defined as "the willingness to give up being the center of my world and accept myself as God's creation," which means I will become lovable, valuable, capable, forgivable, and submissive to God's will. All of us are born with self-centeredness. Our natural tendency is to say, see, and feel that we are the center of the world. Self-centeredness has two primary roots: spiritual and psychological. Its spiritual root is sin. The psychological root is selfishness. We want the world to center around us so we can have what we want when we want it. As babies we need attention, respect, understanding, acceptance, love and a sense of significance, if we are to develop a healthy self-worth. When our development is healthy, we outgrow the narcissistic stage. We come to value others as much as we value ourselves. We allow others to need us as much as we need them. If our development is not healthy, we stay stuck in the stage of self-centeredness.

Nobody surrenders spiritual pride and emotional egotism without the help of loving people. We do not surrender to God without experiencing God's love for us just as we are (Romans 15:7). He makes no demands on us to be more successful, more attractive, or more achieving before He accepts us, loves us, and cares for us (Romans 5:8).

Review Questions

1. What does the book say is the main cause of "low self-worth?"
2. How does God want us to see ourselves?
3. What is the connection between low self-worth and deviancy?
4. What are the values of a nurturing father?
5. What are three important ways to show acceptance?
6. What are the five rules for non-abusive spanking?
7. How would you define "nurturance?"
8. Why does spanking do more harm than good with an adolescent child?

Chapter Six

CREATING POSITIVE COMMUNICATION

Another one of my favorite stories is about the man who noticed one day that his wife wouldn't say anything. She wouldn't answer his questions or respond to his requests. He finally took her to a psychiatrist. After the couple was seated in his office, the psychiatrist noticed that the man's wife would not look up and seemed to be very sad. He asked the husband what he could do to help. The husband replied, "Well doc, my wife seems to be depressed. She won't say anything and she just mopes around the house all the time. I don't know what's wrong with her." The psychiatrist surveyed the situation for a moment and then went over to the woman. He smiled at her and told her how much he appreciated her. She began to perk up. Then he held her hand and told her how pretty she was and she began to smile. He then reached over and gave her a kiss on the cheek and hugged her. She just beamed in response.

When the psychiatrist returned to his desk, he asked the husband if he saw what happened when he walked over and told his wife how much he appreciated her. The husband replied, "Yeah, I saw that." Then the psychiatrist said, "Did you see how she smiled when I held her hand and told her how pretty she looked?" The husband responded, "Yeah, I saw that too!" "Did you see how she beamed when I kissed her on the cheek and hugged her?" "I certainly did see that!" said the husband. "That is what she needs at least three times a week," said the psychiatrist. The husband scratched his head, thought for a moment, then said, "Well doc, I can only bring her in on Tuesdays and Thursdays, but Saturdays are my golf days."

This is a hypothetical, funny story but it has a message for all of us. Positive communication is communication that "cares." When we care what other people are saying and we "validate" their feelings, we are creating positive communication. To "validate" is to give credibility to the feelings of the other person communicating with you, even if you don't agree with him. It doesn't require agreement, just the acknowledgement of the validity of that person's feelings.

It is a fact that poor communication is the number one leadership and management problem. Once understanding breaks down, unity, commitment, motivation, and group activity are lost and the group fails. This is even more of a fact if we see the church as an "organism" rather than an "organization."

Both organisms and organizations have a common goal and the members all work towards that goal. The difference is that an organization does not require that the members work together, but an organism requires that the members be "interdependent." The church is an organism (I Corinthians 12:12-27). Good communication is even more important in an organism. The family structure is basically an organism and positive communication is vital to the family for it to be "functional." A lack of communicating in positive and caring ways is a major defect in dysfunctional families.

Communication Blocks

The Bible gives us instructions on how to create positive communication (Ephesians 4:29-32). We learn from birth to adulthood, how to communicate ideas and concepts and how to persuade and negotiate. We will learn positive ways to do this if our parents teach and model communication that cares.

Unfortunately, we also learn how to distort and confuse our communications so that we do not have to deal with issues head on. Communication distortions are designed to hide from, deflect attention from, hurt or humiliate the other person. It is also important to realize that distorted communication is caused by distorted thoughts. The following are ways to change distorted statements (this material was adapted from unknown sources):

- Sensitize your mind to be able to recognize the distortions when they appear in your thinking and communication.
- Confront each distortion that you recognize, and challenge its accuracy.
- Replace each distorted thought with a truthful and accurate message.
- The most difficult, but most important part, is to communicate the truthful and accurate message to the other person, along

with an appropriate apology for the distorted message and for whatever hurt or damage it might have caused in your relationship.

Remember that all confused or misunderstood communication involves some form of "communication distortion," and the following are some examples:

- TUNNEL VISION – This is when you see only what fits your attitude or state of mind. Thus, you seize on a single, small detail and make that the basis for your overall interpretation. Other important details are deleted or censored from your awareness.

    Example: A couple is going on a picnic for the day. On the way there they have a sharp disagreement over how to get to the park. They finally find it and the rest of the day goes well. But later he complains to her; "you ruined the whole day because of the fight."

- ABSOLUTE STATEMENTS – Absolute statements contain absolute words, such as: "always" or "never" or "can't," etc. These are used to make the argument or statement stronger, but because they are seldom ever true, such statements weaken the truth and are often used to avoid responsibility. These kinds of statements categorize events as "awful" or "terrible" whereas in reality its implications are only mild or moderate.

    Example: Joe forgot to take the garbage out to the street for pickup as he left for work. That night his wife, Marge said furiously, "You always forget to take the garbage out."

- POLARIZED THINKING – In this kind of thinking, everything is either black or white, good or bad, with no other possible explanations in between. Sometimes called "all-or-nothing" thinking, where a person sees only two extreme choices by thinking this way. This thinking seems to have its advantages because you don't have to expend the mental energy to find other options besides the two polarized ones.

Example: Jack phoned his wife Mary at lunchtime and asked her to prepare a fancy, formal dinner for tonight. He had invited the president of the company he works for along with two vice-presidents, and each of their wives to come to his home for dinner. After Mary gets off the phone she thinks, "I don't have the time to do this, but I have to or Jack will threaten to leave me."

- SHOULDS AND OUGHTS – This form of distortion is when a person operates from a list of inflexible rules about how you or other people should act. There is a feeling of rigidity and controlling with this distortion. It also sets people up for "unrealistic expectations" that when unfulfilled, cause frustration and anger.

  Example: Peter comes home from work and tells June that he had a run-in with a fellow worker. Instead of June hearing him out, she immediately starts saying, "You should have just backed away from the fight. You ought to go back right now and apologize to him. You should know better."

- MIND READING – Mind reading can operate in two directions. The first is when you believe that you can tell what the other person is thinking. The second, is when you expect the other person to know what you are thinking, wanting or expecting. Again, it sets us up for unrealistic expectations that distort communication and disrupt relationships.

  Example: Jason and Leah are riding home together in the car. They are both quiet, not talking. Jason is thinking, "I'll bet she is angry at me for not taking out the garbage this morning." She is thinking, "I would sure like to stop at a restaurant. If he loved me, he would know what I want."

- PERSONALIZATION – This distortion is a form of paranoia, inasmuch as the person believes that the actions of other people are directed towards him in a negative way. This is an attitude that reflects a person's insecurities. When we have low self-worth or feel inadequate, we have a tendency to personalize what other people say to us and it then causes us to feel defensive and vengeful. Such distortions are destructive to healthy relationships and tend to create the feeling of alienation.

    Example: When Jill hears her husband Jack singing in the shower, she angrily says, "He does that just because he wants to irritate me."

Examples of Helpful Statements

A. Statements are more helpful if they are…

1. Specific rather that general: "You bumped my cup"; rather than, "You didn't watch where you were going."
2. Tentative rather than absolute: "You seem unconcerned about Jimmy"; rather than, "You don't care about Jimmy and you never will."
3. Informing rather than ordering: "I hadn't finished yet"; rather than, "Stop interrupting me."

B. The most helpful kinds of information are…

1. Behavior descriptions: These report specific acts of the other person that affect you. "I felt like you cut in before I had finished my sentence."
2. Descriptions of your own feelings: "I like what you just said," or "I feel blue."
3. Perception-checking responses: "I thought you weren't interested in trying to understand my idea," or "Are you feeling discouraged?"

C. The least helpful kinds of statements are...

1. <u>Generalizations about the other</u>: "You never pay any attention."
2. <u>Name-calling, trait-labeling</u>: "You're too rude," or "You're a phony."
3. <u>Accusations, imputing undesirable motives to others</u>: "You enjoy putting people down," or "You always have to be the center of attention."
4. <u>Commands and orders</u>: "Don't talk so much," or "Stop laughing."

Five Basic Rules of Communication

1. Be willing to listen and understand others (James 1:19, 20).
2. Be willing to compromise but not on basic convictions (James 3:13-18).
3. Be willing to validate the feelings of others (Romans 15:7).
4. Be willing to be vulnerable with your feelings (James 4:6-10).
5. Be willing to admit when you are wrong and apologize (James 5:16).

Communication Between the Sexes

In his best selling book, "Men Are From Mars, Women Are From Venus," John Gray has successfully made the point that men and women think differently and communicate differently. He states that men are motivated when they feel needed and women are motivated when they feel cherished.

Gray then concludes that when men talk about problems they instinctively offer solutions, but when women talk about problems, they primarily want to be validated. Women are more relationship oriented and men are more goal oriented. It is interesting that the Bible implores men to love their wives and that wives should respect their husbands (Ephesians 5:22-33; Colossians 3:18, 19).

I have found in my ministry that men have the hardest time expressing love to their wives and women have the hardest time showing respect to their husbands. The Bible says, "Husbands, in the same way be considerate as you live with your wives, and treat them with respect as the weaker partner and as heirs with you of the gracious gift of life, so that nothing will hinder your prayers" (I Peter 3:7). Peter is not saying that women are weaker morally or intellectually, but are generally weaker physically and should be cherished and protected.

My experience has proven to me that a man feels "masculine" when he is respected, depended upon, looked up to and thought positively of. A woman feels "feminine" when she is loved, cared for, protected and understood.

Medical studies have shown that between the 18th and 26th week of pregnancy something happens that separates the sexes in a way that forever affects communication between them. Researchers have actually observed testosterone and other sex-related hormones released over a baby boy's brain. This causes changes that happen only to a baby boy.

The sex-related hormones and chemicals that cover the baby boy's brain cause the right side to recede somewhat from the left side. One result is that, in most cases, a boy starts life more "left-brain" oriented. This means that girls start life more "right-brain" oriented than boys or more two-sided in their thinking.[26]

We do know that the left-brain houses more of the logical, analytical, factual and aggressive centers of thought. This is why men are usually more logical, organized and aggressive in their thinking and women are more centered on feelings, language, pictures, fine-detailed work and intuitive thinking. It is quite evident that this can cause communication blocks. There are some natural complications in communication between men and women, which sometimes destroy the validating process.

John Gray concludes that men are fulfilled through working out the details of a problem and women are fulfilled through talking about the problem. "Validating" is the most difficult process in communication for men. Men like to feel that they have the "right" answers and have a difficult time validating a woman's feelings when they disagree with them. As stated before, "validation" does not require that a person agree with someone else's feelings, it only requires that those feelings be recognized as valid to that person.

Communication Requires Openness

Rarely do two people talk openly about their reactions to each other. Most of us withhold our feelings about people (even in relations that are very important or dear to us) because we fear hurting them, making them angry or being rejected by them. Because we don't know how to be open and sensitive, we say nothing. They are then totally unaware of our reactions to them.

Likewise, we continue to be ignorant of how our behavior affects other people. As a result many relationships that could be productive and enjoyable gradually fail under an accumulated load of tiny annoyances, feelings and misunderstandings that were never talked about openly.

Openness must stem from a desire to improve our relationship with others. Openness is not an end in itself but a means to an end. When attempting to elicit an open sharing of reactions to each other, try to convey that you value your relationship and wish to improve it because it is important. We need to strive to know what the other person perceives and feels about our actions and to share what we perceive about theirs.

In the process of communication there must be a willingness to be open to the possibility of risk. Communicating with others usually involves risk. Your willingness to risk your self-esteem, being rejected or hurt by others, etc., depends on the importance of the relationship to you.

Likewise, you cannot expect others to not become angry or feel hurt by your comments. Although the discussion may become intense, spirited, angry or tearful, it should not be coercive or an attempt to force others to change. The attitude should not be to make sure that you win the argument, but rather, "what can each of us learn from this discussion that will make our working together more productive and more satisfying?"

Reactions should be shared as close to the behavior that aroused them as possible so that the other person will know exactly what behavior is being discussed. For example, behavior during the encounter itself can be commented on, e.g., "I feel pushed away when you say those things to me."

Disturbing situations should be discussed as they occur rather than saving up massive accumulations of hurt feelings and annoyances and dumping them on the other all at one time. There should be a "time-out" called by one or the other to allow time for feelings to cool and evaluation as to what needs to be said for clarification. This is when "I messages" are vitally important.

"I messages" allow you the opportunity to be non-accusative, express your feelings and take responsibility for those feelings. Be sure to paraphrase the other's comments about you to make sure you understand him as he intends and check to make sure that he understands you as you intend.

The Process and Development of a Counseling Plan

Present yourself as a serious counselor by setting appointments as is done in professional offices and it will increase the counselee's respect for you and enhance your communication with him.

Set aside a few minutes to prepare for a counseling interview, and avoid the appearance of being interrupted or unprepared. It is important that a counselor practice good physical hygiene and dress appropriately before each counseling session.

The following are suggestions for a counseling session:

1. Your time is valuable; so don't waste it (Ephesians 5:15, 16)!
2. The counselee's time is also important to consider.
3. Because each case is different, handle it differently time wise.
4. The conventional wisdom is that 50 minutes to an hour per session, per week is sufficient. Set a time limit of 10 to 20 weeks for completion.
5. The counselor needs to plan a "closing interview," when it is evident that there is no need to continue further or a referral is necessary.
6. The counselor needs to prepare the counselee for the time when the counseling process will end.
7. The counselor is effective when he convinces his counselees that they are responsible for using the "tools" and "skills" they have learned and will use for the rest of their lives.

The following are steps you can take as a counselor that will be helpful:

1. Have a counselee fill out an information form with specific questions in reference to: date of birth, marriage, occupation, education, family members, examples of abuse (physical, sexual, or substance) and a family history of relationship with parents.
2. It takes time for both the counselor and the counselee to understand the problem; therefore, be patient.

3. The counselee may see the symptoms but fail to grasp the significance of the problem; therefore, don't depend on his/her assessment.
4. Learn to depend on the power of God in the process. God's power is needed in order to change lives (Romans 12:1, 2; I Peter 5:7). Pray daily for yourself and your counselees (I Thessalonians 5:16-18).
5. Allow one or two sessions to diagnose the problem and determine if a referral is necessary.

The following are ways to discover and follow a unique counseling pattern:

1. Use a personality/temperament analysis profile in diagnosing the problem (under the advisement of a professional counselor).
2. Provide an atmosphere conducive to privacy, uninterrupted.
3. Encourage the counselee to express himself/herself freely.
4. Reflect and restate what the counselee says for clarification.
5. Do not register surprise at anything said by the counselee.
6. Refrain from censoring or judging (Romans 15:7).
7. Encourage the counselee to suggest her/his own solutions.
8. Maintain a confidential attitude toward what is discussed.
9. Require the counselee to journal his/her thoughts, feelings and behavior.
10. Give the counselee homework to keep him/her involved in the process between sessions.
11. Avoid attitudes of "labeling," "condemning," "blaming," and "rejecting."
12. When recommending solutions, be willing to use the Bible as your standard of authority.

Counseling Techniques

The following list will help the counselor to be professional and confidential:

1. Be cautious, both publicly and privately, when handling confidential information (which should be kept in a locked storage unit).
2. Do not talk about other counselors or counselees.

3. Counsel in appropriate places, such as an office that is private and allows for security and confidentiality, in order to control distractions (with someone nearby to provide monitoring).

The following are recommended techniques in counseling that provide a positive and effective interview with the counselee:

1. Give the counselee your undivided attention.
2. Develop good listening skills.
3. Look for vital pieces of information that will help you diagnose the problem (look cautiously into the counselee's past for clues).
4. Concentrate on listening and asking questions to clarify thought.
5. Avoid asking questions with "Yes" or "No" answers.
6. Ask questions that require answers that are informative and relative to the problem.
7. Ask questions such as the following:
   a. "When were you aware of the problem?"
   b. "What did you feel when you recognized the problem?"
   c. "How would you describe the problem?"
   d. "Where else have you looked for help?"
   e. "How has your family responded to the problem?"
   f. "How has the problem impacted your life?"
   g. "What do you think could be a possible solution to the problem?"
   h. "How have you tried to cope with it?"
8. Do not endanger the relationship by trying to force information out of the counselee.
9. Allow the counselee to develop at a pace according to his comfort level.
10. Take notes at each session, recording the "presenting problem" and all pertinent information revealed by the counselee.

Feelings are to the counselor what symptoms are to the medical doctor. The counselor needs to provide the counselee with a supportive environment in which the counselee can feel free to express his/her feelings. The purpose of expressing feelings is to help locate and diagnose the problem (observing body language is also important in the process of determining the problem).

Counselees are often motivated to seek help because of strong emotions like prolonged sadness, emptiness, guilt, inadequacy, shame, anger, hurt, fear, anxiety and confusion. The counselor should not try to convince the counselee that he or she should not feel that way (validation is important here).

Review Questions

1. What is the most important aspect of positive communication?
2. How would you define "communication blocks?"
3. What are the five basic rules of communication?
4. Why is a counseling plan necessary in counseling others?
5. What is the most important symptom in diagnosing a problem?
6. Why shouldn't a counselor ask "yes" or "no" questions?
7. What is a "closing interview?"
8. Why is openness important in communication?

Chapter Seven

BASIC PRINCIPLES OF CRISIS INTERVENTION

When we think of a crisis we may think of a problem that has interrupted our lives for a brief period and after some problem solving, will go away. The "Crisis Counseling" we are talking about is really "Crisis Intervention!" What is crisis intervention? "It is entering into the life situation of an individual or family to alleviate the impact of a crisis in order to help mobilize the resources of those directly affected."[27]

A crisis of this level or magnitude can manifest a problem that has gone on for some time and the crisis itself may be the tip of the iceberg. It may reflect a deeper problem that has not been dealt with or has been denied. The following information details Crisis Intervention:

Defining a Crisis

1. It can be a turning point in a person's life.
2. It is "a subjective reaction to a stressful life experience, one so affecting the stability of the individual that the ability to cope or function may be seriously compromised."[28]
3. The crisis is not the situation itself; rather, it is the person's perception of and response to the situation.

What Are the Characteristics of a Person in Crisis?

1. Perceiving a precipitating event as being meaningful and threatening.
2. Appearing unable to modify or lessen the impact of stress.
3. Experiencing increased fear, tension, and/or confusion.
4. Proceeding rapidly to an active state of crisis – a state of disequilibrium.

General Observations about Crisis Theory

1. Temporary upset, accompanied by some confusion and disorganization and characterized by a person's inability to cope with a specific situation through the use of traditional problem-solving methods.
2. Occurs episodically during the normal life span of a person.
3. Neither an illness nor a pathological experience; reflects a realistic struggle in the individual's current life situation.
4. Time span between precipitating event and final resolution varies, usually four to six weeks.

DOMESTIC VIOLENCE

<u>Types of Domestic Violence</u>

- Physical Abuse
- Emotional Abuse
- Sexual Abuse
- Destruction of Property

EXAMPLE: <u>Understanding The Domestic Violence Law in Washington State</u>

1. It is against the law to hit, shove, push, pinch, grab, restrain, etc., an intimate partner.
2. It is not necessary for the partner to press charges – the state presses charges.
3. Many times a "no-contact order" is involved; no contact means "NO" contact, even through a third party.
4. Anyone convicted of domestic violence must complete a one-year state approved counseling program.

NOTE: Many times in the church, women have been told to go back home and "submit." To those spiritual leaders and others who give that advice, I have some advice: Set the example. Demonstrate Christ-likeness and take the beating for that woman. If you are not willing to do that, then do not suggest it.

General Observations about Batterers

1. They come in all shapes and forms – rich and poor, educated and uneducated, raised in the church and no relation to the church.
2. Without intervention, three trends are common:
   a. The cycle of abuse accelerates.
   b. The battering becomes more serious.
   c. The abuser feels less and less remorse.
3. They tend to be isolated.
4. Drugs and alcohol are contributing factors in much domestic violence but are not the cause of the abuse.
5. They attempt to maintain control by intimidation.
6. Expect minimization and denial: "She drove me to it. It's her fault."
7. They have rigid belief systems regarding the role of women.

General Observations about Victims

1. Many times they are ambivalent and blame themselves.
2. They lack the resources to leave the abusive situation.
3. They need a safe place to go, if they choose to leave.
4. They too often think they can change the abuser.
5. Although they have an intuitive sense of the danger level, they misjudge the danger frequently.

Helping to End Domestic Violence

1. Believe the victim and take him/her seriously. You might be the first person to actually believe him/her.
2. Do not encourage marriage counseling in an abusive relationship. It puts the victim in more danger. It is the abuser's problem. Couple counseling is appropriate after all the safety issues are addressed.
3. Remember, it is the victim's decision to stay or go. Be there to provide the emotional support needed for the victim to make a decision.
4. The number one issue is the safety of the victim.
5. Encourage the victim to have a safety plan – escape route, phone numbers, extra car keys, money, children's birth certificates, etc., in an easily accessible location.

6. The best modality for treating a batterer is group counseling; the minimum length of counseling should be 26 weekly sessions.
7. The abuser's belief system needs to change.
8. Train children at home and in the church that battering is wrong, that the Bible does not condone it and that the church will not tolerate it.

DEPRESSION/SUICIDE

A depressed mood may be, in itself, a normal phenomenon. After an experience of loss or an experience that hurts an individual's self-esteem, a sense of futility and lowered self-worth is to be expected (II Corinthians 4:4-10; I Thessalonians 4:13-18). The depression is an attempt to overcome or "repair" the loss. In many cases it is a coping mechanism a person engages in as an attempt to escape reality.

Causes of Depression

1. Poor eating habits and/or not enough rest.
2. Reaction to drugs (toxic depression) or physical causes.
3. Repressed anger and anger turned inward.
4. Reactive or grief depression.
5. Negative thought patterns of faulty thinking.
6. A physiological abnormality creating a chemical imbalance.

Loss and Change

Loss is one of the major themes underlying depression. Real or perceived loss is often the cause of depression. Loss becomes a trigger for depression.

Steps in Helping to Lift Depression

1. RAPPORT – building a rapport in the form of simple questions:

    a. "How long have you felt this way?"
    b. "When do you remember this starting?"
    c. "How frequently do you have episodes of depression?"

       d. "How long do the episodes last?"
       e. "When have you experienced this mood before?"
       f. "What pattern do you see in these episodes?"
       g. "What did you do to help yourself?"
       h. "What are the options you have to handle this?"
       i. "What is the worst thing you can imagine happening?"
       j. "What are you doing to make yourself depressed?"
       k. "What are you thinking about that is bringing on depression?"

2. REASSURANCE – creating reassurance and avoiding shortcuts:

       a. Make every effort to keep the depressed person active.
       b. Ask, "If you were not depressed, what would you do?"
       c. Make specific plans of activity.

3. REVELATION – while he/she is learning, help the depressed person look at all sides of this new information he/she is receiving.

4. REORGANIZATION – help this person to develop a thorough understanding of the cause of depression and construct a stronger self-concept:

       a. Keep up a daily routine.
       b. Get out of the house – go somewhere.
       c. See family and friends often but in small doses.
       d. Exercise.
       e. If it is difficult to talk, write.
       f. Let people know you need encouragement, not scolding.
       g. Remember depression usually ends.
       h. Keep up a good diet.
       i. Have someone you can complain to and express your anger.
       j. Work on your negative self-talk.

Diagnostic Criteria for Major Depressive Episode
(Adapted from the Diagnostic and Statistical Manual of Mental Disorders)

A. At least five of the following symptoms have been present during the same two-week period and represent a change from previous functioning (at least one of the symptoms is a depressed mood, and the other, a loss of interest or pleasure):
   1. Depressed mood (or can be irritable mood in children and adolescents) most of the day, nearly every day.
   2. Markedly diminished interest or pleasure in all, or almost all, activities most of the day, nearly every day.
   3. Significant weight loss or weight gain when not dieting (more than 5% of body weight in a month), or decrease or increase in appetite every day.
   4. Insomnia or hypersomnia nearly every day.
   5. Psychomotor agitation or retardation nearly every day.
   6. Fatigue or loss of energy nearly every day.
   7. Feelings of worthlessness or excessive or inappropriate guilt every day.
   8. Diminished ability to think or concentrate, or indecisiveness every day.
   9. Recurrent thoughts of death (not just a fear of dying), recurrent suicide ideation without a specific plan, or a suicide attempt or a specific plan for committing suicide.

B. The following are facts that must be considered in the diagnostic process:
   1. It cannot be established that an organic factor initiated and maintained the depression.
   2. The depression is not a normal reaction to the death of a loved one.

Dealing with Suicidal Tendencies

Warning Signals!

* Any previous suicide attempt.
* Verbal suicide threats.
* Moodiness or depression.
* Taking unnecessary risks.
* Loss of interest in work/school.
* Sudden tendency toward isolation.
* Getting affairs in order: giving away personal possessions or making a will.
* A preoccupation with death and/or after life.
* Formulation of a suicide plan.
* Significant changes in sleeping or eating patterns.

What to do ...

* Take the person's threat SERIOUSLY.
* Be DIRECT; talk openly.
* Let the person know you care.
* Ask how the person is feeling and inquire whether he or she has a specific suicide plan.
* Make a suicide contract (an agreement with a person not to hurt him/herself).
* Urge a person to get professional help; have them call their local crisis line.

The Stress Scale of Adjusting to Change
(Check the events that have happened to you in the past 12 months)

Event	Value	Score	Event	Value	Score
Death of a Spouse	100	__	Son or daughter leave home	29	__
Divorce	73	__	Trouble with in-laws	29	__
Marital Separation	65	__	Outstanding personal achievement	28	__
Jail Term	63	__	Wife begins or stops work	26	__
Death of a close family member	63	__	Begin or end school	26	__
Personal injury or illness	53	__	Change in living conditions	25	__
Marriage	50	__	Revision of personal habits	24	__
Fired at work	47	__	Trouble with boss	23	__
Marital reconciliation	45	__	Change in work hours, conditions	20	__
Retirement	45	__	Change in residence	20	__
Change in family member's health	44	__	Change in schools	20	__

Pregnancy	40__	Change in recreational habits	19__
Sex difficulties	39__	Change in church activities	19__
Addition to family	39__	Change in social activities	18__
Business readjustment	39__	Mortgage or loan under $10,000	17__
Change in financial status	38__	Change in sleeping habits	16__
Death of a close friend	37__	Change in # of family gatherings	15__
Change to different line of work	36__	Change in eating habits	15__
Change in # of arguments w/ mate	35__	Vacation	13__
Mortgage or loan over $10,000	31__	Christmas season	12__
Foreclosure of mortgage or loan	30__	Minor violations of the law	11__
Change in work responsibilities	29__		

According to the two doctors, Holmes and Rahe, if your score is under 150 stress units, you have only 37 percent chance of getting sick or becoming depressed within the next two years because of the amount of change in your life.

If your score is between 150 and 300, the probability rises to 51 percent. And if your score is over 300, the odds are 4 to 5 (80 percent) that you could become ill or depressed during the next two years because of the amount of change in your life.

This test is widely used, especially in the military, to predict whether one will be sick during the subsequent two years.[29]

SEXUAL ABUSE

Definitions

- Covert Incest – meets the sexual desires of the parents.
- Emotional Incest – meets the emotional needs of the parents.

An Overview

1. 75% of all reported cases involve stepfather/daughter or father/daughter incest.
2. Sexual abuse occurs most often between the ages of 7-12 but is common earlier.
3. All victims are coerced and manipulated by the power imbalance, although most perpetrators do not use violence.
4. 40% of all victims require therapy in adulthood.

Risk Factors and Preconditions for Child Sexual Abuse

1. The presence of a stepfather in the victim's family.
2. The victim has always lived with the mother.
3. The victim was not close to his/her mother.
4. The victim's mother never finished high school.
5. The victim had no physical affection from his/her father.
6. The victim's family income was usually under $15,000.
7. The victim had two or fewer friends in childhood.

The Grooming Process in Father/Daughter Incest

1. A trust factor is developed between the daughter and father.
2. There is favoritism of the father to the daughter.
3. There is usually alienation of the father and mother.
4. The grooming and seducing process is always done in secret.
5. The normal boundaries between father and daughter are violated in areas of:
   - bathing
   - dressing
   - bathroom behavior
   - conversations
6. The grooming phase results in stages of child sexual abuse.

Stages of Child Sexual Abuse

1. Engagement: access and opportunity, relationship, inducements.
2. Sexual Interaction Phase: escalation of engagement.
3. Secrecy develops.
4. Disclosure and sexual intimacy develops.

Summary of the Grooming Process Cues

1. The perpetrator will build a unique kind of trust; usually accompanied by favors.
2. The abuser develops alienation of the victim from family members and peers.

3. Then the abuser demands secrecy upon the victim.
4. Then the abuser continues in boundary violations.

Diagnostic Criteria for Sexual Addiction
(The presence of FIVE or MORE of the following reflect sexual addiction)

1. Sexual obsession and fantasy is a primary coping strategy.
2. Sexual behavior is the central organizing principle of daily life.
3. Inordinate amounts of time spent in obtaining sex, being sexual, or recovering from sexual experience.
4. Amount or duration of sexual behavior often exceeds what the person intended.
5. Severe mood shifts around sexual acting out.
6. Escalating pattern of increasing amounts of sexual experience because the current level of activity is no longer sufficient (exemplified by more of current sexual behavior or addition of new sexual behavior or initiation of new high risk, illicit, and immoral behavior).
7. Persistent pursuit of self-destructive or high-risk sexual behavior.
8. Persistent desire or efforts to limit sexual behavior.
9. Inability to stop behavior despite adverse consequences.
10. Pattern of out-of-control (compulsive) sexual activity for two years.
11. Pattern of alternating excessive control and out-of-control behavior for five years.
12. Severe consequences due to sexual behavior.
13. Presence of clear hierarchy of sexual acting out behavior.
14. Important social, occupational or recreational activities sacrificed or reduced because of sexual behavior.
15. Presence of any three of the following associated conditions:
    - extreme sexual shame
    - other addictions
    - has been or is currently victim of sexual abuse
    - secret or "double life" due to sexual behavior
    - sexualizing of nurturing
    - few or no non-sexual relationships
    - suicidal ideation or attempt
    - presence of sex-negative behavior
    - excessive reliance on denial
    - presence of co-dependent personality disorder

DEALING WITH GRIEF

Grief that reflects a loss: Death of a child – loss of the future; Death of a spouse – loss of the present; Death of a parent – loss of the past.

Stages of Grief

Dr Elisabeth Kubler-Ross concluded that dying people usually go through five stages as a way of healing deep hurt.[30]

STAGE:	IN DYING	IN DEALING WITH GRIEF
Denial	I don't ever admit I will die	I don't admit I am hurting
Anger	I blame others for letting death hurt and destroy me	I blame others for hurting and destroying me
Bargaining	I set up conditions to be fulfilled before I'm ready to die	I set up conditions to be fulfilled before I'm ready to forgive
Depression	I blame myself for letting death destroy me	I blame myself for letting the loss destroy me
Acceptance	I look forward to dying	I look forward to growth from the loss

Signs of Unresolved Grief

1. They refuse to talk about the deceased.
2. On anniversaries/birthdays they experience depression.
3. They constantly compare new relationships with old.
4. They experience morbid grief (Example: keeping ashes of loved ones).
5. There is excessive grave visitation or never visiting.

The Nature of Grief

1. No one can get through life without loss and grief.
2. Grief is a God-given natural, healthy, self-corrective process whereby an individual can separate from someone or something that has been lost.

3. It is healthier to express emotions than to repress them. Repression is the means by which intolerable memories are kept out of the consciousness.
4. Anger is a common response to loss.
5. Guilt is a normal and common reaction as well. No one succeeds at being good and loving all the time. Usually there is a sense of unfinished business.
6. Pain must be faced before it can be healed. The grieving person will relive memories and only gradually confront each one with the realization that it no longer corresponds to something real. The whole sequence is repeated over and over. The specific psychological task is to break the emotional tie one has with the deceased so he/she can reinvest attachment and emotional energy in people.
7. There is no time limit to grief. He/she can get "stuck" in a stage of grief.

Responding to Grief

DO'S

1. Acknowledge the loss with a call, card, or letter.
2. Simply say, "I'm sorry," or "Words fail me."
3. Words aren't always necessary – hugs, tears, etc., convey sympathy.
4. Give the mourner permission to grieve.
5. Listen without being judgmental.
6. Allow the person to talk about the deceased loved one.
7. Ask open-ended questions.
8. Offer practical advice and to pray with them.
9. Share a pleasant memory or words of admiration for the deceased.
10. Remember them on the painful holidays, especially the "firsts."
11. Remember that grief is long lasting.
12. Remember that usually the most difficult time is 7-9 months later.
13. Remember that nothing you can say will stop the person's pain.

DON'TS

1. Don't say, "Don't cry" or "Be brave." This may cause repression.
2. Don't use clichés – "Time heals all wounds" or "The Lord knows best."

3. Don't be afraid of tears.
4. Don't say, "I know how you feel."
5. Don't make statements or ask questions that induce guilt or affix blame.
6. Don't change the subject when the person talks about his/her loved one.
7. Don't tell the grieving person his/her loss is God's will.
8. Don't try to answer the question, "Why?"
9. Don't attempt to minimize the loss because others are still in the family unit.
10. Don't encourage the person to "get over it" because of your discomfort.

Grief is not the result of what happened to the deceased but what happened to the bereaved. Loss of self happens when someone significant dies (Example: when the wife dies, loss of meaning in life as a husband).

The core of grief is anxiety. It is a form of separation anxiety. Resolving grief is learning to live with the memories, both positive and negative and to restore meaning to life.

CHEMICAL ADDICTION

Chemical addiction is a primary, progressive, complex addiction of psycho-physiological characteristics, identified by dependence on substance or substances and resulting in habitual (compulsive) use without regard to life's consequences.

Early-Stage Alcoholism

Blackouts, gulping drinks, sneaking drinking, repeated attempts at abstinence, increasing tolerance, drinking before drinking functions, preoccupation with alcohol, uncomfortable in non-alcoholic situations, irritation in discussing drinking, frequent reference to alcohol in normal conversation.

Mid-Stage Alcoholism

Changing beverage of choice, loss of interest in activities not related to drink, job loss or frequent job changes, projection, denial, alibis, neglect of food, loss of control, protects the supply, avoids family and friends, inappropriately plans large life changes.

Late-Stage Alcoholism

Tremors, early morning drinks, physical deterioration, onset of lengthy intoxication, moral deterioration, impaired thinking, drinking with inferiors, unable to initiate action, indefinable fears, all alibis exhausted.

The Twelve Steps of Alcoholics Anonymous
(Bill Wilson and the Oxford Group (1930's) developed these steps)

1. We admitted we were powerless over alcohol – that our lives had become unmanageable.
2. Came to believe that a Power greater than ourselves could restore us to sanity.
3. Made a decision to turn our will and our lives over to the care of God, as we understood him.
4. Made a searching and fearless moral inventory of ourselves.
5. Admitted to God, to ourselves, and to another human being the exact nature of our wrongs.
6. Were entirely ready to have God remove all these defects of character.
7. Humbly asked Him to remove our shortcomings.
8. Made a list of all persons we had harmed and became willing to make amends to them all.
9. Made direct amends to such people whenever possible except when to do so would injure them or others.
10. Continued to take personal inventory and when we were wrong, promptly admitted it.
11. Sought through prayer and meditation to improve our conscious contact with God, as we understood him, praying only for knowledge of his will for us and the power to carry that out.
12. Having had a spiritual awakening as a result of these steps, we tried to carry this message to alcoholics, and to practice these principles in all our affairs.

Observations on Helping the Chemically Dependent

1. When observing a major change in the personality of someone, always screen for drugs and alcohol first.
2. Remember the rules of an alcoholic home:
   - Don't talk, Don't feel, Don't trust
3. The premier defense mechanism is denial. This fortress has to be assaulted at the belief system. The inconsistencies must be confronted.
4. Expect grandiose thinking.
5. Expect all or nothing thinking.
6. Do not be surprised at long periods of sobriety. That does not indicate a "cure."
7. In recovery, expect relapses. But do not give up helping.
8. Chemical addiction stunts personality growth. Ascertain when the person first started using – that is where the person is in maturity and in coping skills.
9. Remember that the whole family needs help. As the addicted person begins recovery, do not neglect to see that all family members receive help. Co-dependency is the nature of this family. The family system needs help as well as the substance abuser.

The Essence of Crisis Intervention

Once a crisis event has been identified and you feel comfortable that it is the major precipitating factor, the Skilled Helper should work toward understanding how this event is perceived. As some professionals have noted, the crisis does not lie directly in the event, but is the result of the interpretation of it and the interaction between the person and the event.

The perception of the counselee and the kinds of messages given to him about the event produce the crisis. Due to intense emotions, the person may be blinded to resources or possible solutions. As a part of the assessment, the counselor will need to gain information that will allow him to suggest creative resources or alternatives for action that the counselee has not considered.

A Skilled Helper is not required to be a professional, only to be equipped, trained, compassionate and involved in people's lives. The essence of crisis intervention is the helper's concern for the spiritual and emotional welfare of people.

The Skilled Helper must be willing to sacrifice time and perhaps money or whatever, to make sure people are comforted through counseling and are able to understand what is happening to them, and who they need to turn to for "divine" help.

It is not an easy task, but one that can be greatly rewarding and requires of us as Christians the willingness to "love our neighbors as ourselves."

Review Questions

1. How would you define "Crisis Intervention?"
2. What are the types of "domestic violence?"
3. What is the "grooming process" in sexual abuse cases?
4. What are the five "Stages of Grief" by Kubler-Ross?
5. What is the nature of "addiction?"
6. How would you assess an event that has caused a crisis?
7. What are the three stages of alcoholism?
8. Why is step one of the 12 steps of Alcoholics Anonymous so important?

Chapter Eight

THE AUTHORITY AND RELIABILITY OF SCRIPTURE

When we think in terms of counseling others, we need to again revisit the "authority and reliability of Scripture." For the true believer, the thought of the Bible being anything other than "word for word" inspired of God, is an unrealistic concept. As a counselor, who relies on the Bible as his/her final authority, the truth of the Scriptures is fact and has application to every facet of our lives. The apostle Paul said, "All Scripture is God-breathed and is useful for teaching, rebuking, correcting and training in righteousness, so that the man of God may be thoroughly equipped for every good work" (II Timothy 3:16, 17). We believe that the Scriptures give us the knowledge we need to live by and to counsel others in all aspects of life.

The Bible was written over a period of some sixteen hundred years with some forty different writers being used. These men lived in different eras separated by millenniums, in different sections of the world, coming from differing backgrounds. Yet, when all of their writings are put together, there is an amazing harmonious, united whole, without a single solitary proven contradiction to be found therein.

There have been men and women who have made attempts to find contradictions in the Bible. However, all such attempts have been easily dissipated. It has been proven that all so-called contradictions have not been substantiated when there is: (1) the understanding of exactly what a contradiction is, and (2) the studying of the matter at hand in a more minute and careful way.

We must keep in mind that a contradiction exists when two statements cannot both be true, not because they differ. Two statements cannot rightfully be pronounced contradictory if on any rational basis, we may suppose them both to be true. If it is possible for both statements to be true, then it is possible that no contradiction exists. If it is probable that both statements are true, then it is probable that no contradiction exists.

Thus, in the case of the two accounts of the demon-possessed men, one of them was probably the prominent speaker, and that is possibly the reason he alone is mentioned in Mark's and Luke's account (Matthew 8:28, 29; Mark 5:1-10; Luke 8:26-39).

The Proven Accuracy of The Bible

Regardless of how far science has advanced, or may advance, the Bible has never been proven obsolete nor has a scientific discrepancy been discovered. In 1861, the French Academy of Science published fifty-one facts, all of which contradicted the Scriptures, it was thought. However, none of these, so-called facts, is accepted as true today by a living man (recognized authority) of science.

The Bible has always been accurate historically. The nation of the Hittites is an example of the claim of skeptics that the Bible is not accurate historically. There are many references to the Hittites in the Old Testament Scriptures (Genesis 15:20; Exodus 3:8, 17; Numbers 13:29; Deuteronomy 20:17; Joshua 1:4).

For years skeptics of various kinds have denied the historical existence of such a nation. But, the archaeologist's spade uncovered evidence that indisputably proved that such a nation of people did exist. In the Egyptian's ruins, which have been discovered, the Hittites were mentioned in an inscription at the tomb of Merneptha (the supposed Pharaoh of the Exodus).

The same thing can be said of the existence of Belshazzar the king of Babylon in Daniel's day (Daniel 5). The historical evidence in our possession had no reference of him as a king of Babylon and therefore the skeptics have had a field day with this one. Unbelieving scholars said that Nabonidus was king of Babylon at the time of its fall and not Belshazzar. They took the position that Belshazzar was never king, and doubted he even existed.

It is true that over a hundred years ago our historical sources (outside of the Bible) showed that Nabonidus was the last king of Babylon and was not killed when the city was taken by the Persians, but was given a pension by his conquerors. Records discovered by archaeologists in the middle of the 19th century discovered a great number of clay tablets that were excavated in the region, which was ancient Babylonia, and were sent to the British Museum.

During the last half of the nineteenth century many scholars examined these tablets and came to the conclusion that Belshazzar was actually co-ruler with his father, Nabonidus. This is the reason for the biblical reference to Belshazzar as the number two ruler and his offer to make Daniel number three. The clay tablets show us the reason for the raising of Belshazzar to the position of ruling monarch – namely, because of the absence of his father from Babylon who was in Persia growing his garden.

The Bible is sometimes "Pre-Historic." In the Book of Isaiah, the prophet names the king of Persia, Cyrus, before he was ever born (Isaiah 45:1; II Chronicles 36:22, 23). Isaiah wrote his prophecies around 700 B.C. and Cyrus was born around 590 B.C.

There is in the "Dead Sea Scrolls" (discovered in the mid-twentieth century) a complete scroll of the Book of Isaiah dated around 150 B.C. The earliest manuscripts (copies of copies of the original), in our possession, are dated around 900 A.D. That means that this Dead Sea scroll of Isaiah was copied 1,000 years before the earliest manuscript in our possession. Scholars tell us that this scroll differs only in a few minor details from the earliest manuscript in our possession copied a thousand years later.

What does this tell us of the providence of God, who maintained the integrity of the Scriptures (there must have been thousands of handwritten copies on parchment made during that time) from the originals to our time? It says that the Scriptures are reliable and the true Word of God. The Jews, with God's help, evidently did a fabulous job transmitting the Old Testament Scriptures down to us through the centuries (Romans 3:1, 2).

The Bible is Accurate Geographically

Anytime the Bible says a given location is in the South, it is always in the south! Anytime the Bible says a given place is up, it is always in that given direction. When the angel of the Lord spoke to Philip and said, "Arise, and go toward the south unto the way that goeth down from Jerusalem, unto Gaza: the same is desert" (Acts 8:26; ASV). That is the way it was, geographically. Gaza was south of Jerusalem. Furthermore, the way did go "down." The terrain from Jerusalem to Gaza is from the mountains to the seacoast; hence, downward.

The Bible has never been proven to be inaccurate scientifically, historically, geographically or any other way. Archaeology continues to support the Bible, and we believe it will always do so. The assumption that a document is inaccurate because it mentions a fact that has not been confirmed by scholars is the height of arrogance.

The Bible is Divinely Inspired

The Old Testament foretold that Jesus would be betrayed by a friend and ultimately rejected (Psalm 41:9; Isaiah 53:1-3). His price would be thirty pieces of silver and during the course of His trial He would be spit upon and beaten (Zechariah 11:12; Isaiah 50:6). As to the mode of His death, His hands and feet would be pierced through and none of His bones were to be broken (Psalm 22:16; Exodus 12:46). While dying He would thirst and be given vinegar to drink (Psalm 22:15; 69:21). In death Jesus would be numbered with transgressors (outcasts) and buried with the rich. Though dead, His flesh would not see corruption, rather, He would be raised from the dead and exalted to the right hand of God (Isaiah 53:1-9; Psalm 16:10; 110:1; Acts 2:22-36).

It is remarkable that all these prophecies were fulfilled in Jesus centuries later. It only takes a survey of the historical records of Matthew, Mark, Luke and John to see how wonderfully all the prophecies were fulfilled (II Peter 1:19-21).

Peter W. Stoner, the mathematician, states that just selecting eight Old Testament prophecies describing the coming of Christ proves that the odds are astounding that they would be fulfilled. He estimates that the odds of these being accidentally fulfilled by any one person (as Christ did) are approximately 1 to 10^{17} (that's a one followed by seventeen zeros)[31]

The New Testament Text

There are over 4,000 Greek manuscripts (copies) of the New Testament in existence today in whole or in part (some dated in the 4th and 5th century). Along with the manuscripts there are several versions of the New Testament, which are translations of the New Testament into languages other than Greek. These versions are dated from the 1st century to the 4th century.

There are quotations from post-apostolic writers, who are called "Church Fathers," that are of considerable value in determining the text of the New Testament. Some of these writers were very close to being, and some were, contemporaries of the apostles. The accumulation of the manuscript evidence has been so vast and the work of the scientific textual critic has been so precise, that we may express complete confidence in the reliability of the New Testament Text.

While it is true that some minor manuscript variations exist, they are negligible. The Greek scholars, Westcott and Hort, felt that the debatable portions of the New Testament Text could hardly amount to more than a thousandth part of the whole. The New Testament documents have been in existence over 1,900 years. For fifteen of those centuries they were copied by hand. In spite of the copies being done by hand for several centuries, there are only some twelve to twenty significant textual variations in the entire New Testament Text, and none of these affects an important doctrinal matter.

In comparison, if we consider the works of William Shakespeare, his writings have considerable problems. Shakespeare's writings have existed less than four centuries (and since the invention of the printing press) and yet, "in every one of Shakespeare's thirty-seven plays there are probably a hundred readings in dispute, a large number of which materially affect the meaning of the passages in which they occur."[32]

F.F. Bruce, Professor of Biblical Criticism and Exegesis in the University of Manchester, has stated: "The evidence for our New Testament writings is ever so much greater than the evidence for many writings of classical authors, the authenticity of which no one dreams of questioning. And if the New Testament were a collection of secular writings, their authenticity would generally be regarded as beyond all doubt. It is a curious fact that historians have often been much readier to trust the New Testament records than have many theologians..."[33]

"Perhaps we can appreciate how wealthy the New Testament is in manuscript attestation if we compare the textual material for other ancient historical works. For Caesar's 'Gallic War' (composed between 58 and 50 B.C.) there are several extant (still existing, not extinct, lost or destroyed) manuscripts, but only nine or ten are good, and the oldest is some 900 years later than Caesar's day. Of the 142 books of the Roman History of Livy (59 B.C.-A.D. 17) only thirty-five survive, these are known to us from not more than twenty manuscripts of any consequence, only one of which, and that containing fragments of books 3-6, as old as the fourth century."[34]

Plenary Verbal Inspiration

The word "plenary" means, "complete in all aspects or essentials," and the word "verbal" means, "of, relating to, or associated with words."[35] It is very important while discussing the inspiration of the Bible to understand what that term means, and how it is interpreted or understood by others.

There are those who suggest that the inspiration of the Bible is merely that of "natural genius." By this they mean that the Bible is purely the result of superior spiritual insight on the part of natural man (such as Shakespeare). Others allege that the Bible is "partially inspired." Advocates of this position say that the spiritual portions of Scripture are inspired, but such does not extend to historical, scientific, or geographical facts as presented in the Bible. Also we find the assertion that the "concepts" or "ideas" of Scripture are inspired but not the "words" themselves (this is the most popular today).

Christ himself believed in the "word for word" (plenary verbal) inspiration of the Scriptures. The "jot" was the smallest Hebrew letter, and the "tittle" was a tiny projection on certain Hebrew letters. Yet, the Lord affirms the minutest accuracy for the whole of the Old Testament (Matthew 5:17, 18).

Jesus engaged the Sadducees in debate concerning the resurrection of the dead – a doctrine, which they denied. He charged them with ignorance of the Scriptures and then made an argument, which depended entirely upon the very "tense" of the verb form "to be." He was implying that when God said to Moses, "I am the God of Abraham, Isaac, and Jacob," ("I am" being in the present tense) these men were still alive many years after they died physically (Exodus 3:6).

Unless the Old Testament Scriptures are verbally inspired, Christ argued in vain. His opponents were silenced (Matthew 22:31-33). Jesus proclaimed to God the Father and to the whole world that His authority came from God and that His words were God's words. This passage confirms that Jesus believed that the words He spoke came directly from God and that there was no intermediary or interpretation of man in the process (John 12:47-50; 17:8).

King David once said, "The Spirit of Jehovah spoke through me; his word was on my tongue" (II Samuel 23:2). David did not say that God's "thoughts" were in his mind, or the Lord's "concepts," but God's "word" was upon his tongue. The apostle Paul said that the things of God revealed to him were revealed by the Spirit, and that the words he received from God were divine revelation. He stated that these words were Spirit-directed words not words of mere human wisdom. He said, "This is what we speak, not in words taught us by human wisdom but in words taught by the Spirit, expressing spiritual truths in spiritual words" (I Corinthians 2:13). The inspiration of God blended well with the mind, outlook, temperament, interests, literary habits, and stylistic idiosyncrasies of each writer.

In the New Testament the apostle Paul said, "All Scripture is inspired by God..." (II Timothy 3:16 NASB) The Scriptures, therefore, consist of divinely directed communications, to certain commissioned persons, written down, authenticated by miracles, and made available to the world (Hebrews 2:3, 4). The word INSPIRATION comes from the Greek word, "theopneustos," which is a compound word formed from the word for "God" (Theos) and the word meaning, "to breathe" (pneo). Thus, Paul is actually saying that the Scriptures are "God-breathed!" The Bible is quite literally, then, the WORD OF GOD!

The word "scripture" comes from an old Latin word that means, "writing". As used in II Timothy 3:16, the word refers to the sacred writings of men inspired of God. We notice that the body of writing involved is – "all Scripture." Paul was specifically referring to the writings of the Old Testament in this verse, but in a broader sense it must include all "writings" of the nature proven to be inspired.

By the time of Emperor Constantine of Rome (306-337 A.D.), the 27 books of the New Testament were being used and accepted by the churches as being inspired. The entire 66 books of the Bible were officially "canonized" (meaning, "a measuring line, or rule to go by") and accepted as authentically inspired by God, at the Council of Carthage in 397 A.D.[36]

The apostle Peter stated, "But know this first of all, that no prophecy of Scripture is a matter of one's own interpretation, for no prophecy was ever made by an act of human will, but men moved by the Holy Spirit spoke from God" (II Peter 1:20, 21; NASB).

These verses confirm the fact that God, through his Holy Spirit, did not give an idea to a prophet and let him interpret it and then put it into his own words and give it to others. Peter is saying that the Holy Spirit used the unique vocabulary and linguistic ability of each prophet and chose the words each would use to express the thoughts that God wanted expressed. And Paul confirms this as fact (I Corinthians 2:12, 13).

Objections to Plenary Verbal Inspiration

The following are the most common objections to verbal inspiration:

1. Objection: "If the Old Testament was verbally inspired, New Testament writers would not have quoted it as carelessly as they did."

- Answer: such quotations are attempts by the Holy Spirit to take the basic truths of the Old Testament passage and give it amplification and meaning in its New Testament context (i.e. Isaiah 11:10; Romans 15:12).

2. Objection: "There are scientific errors in the Bible which would not be there if it were verbally inspired of God."

    - Answer: A scientific discrepancy can only exist when there is a conflict between a proven fact of science and an explicit statement of Scripture.
        1) We are not obliged to defend either scientific "theory" (or more likely hypothesis) or theological speculation.
        2) So-called scientific mistakes are either unproved theory or a misinterpretation of Scripture.

3. Objection: "Since there are historical errors in the Bible which, if the Bible were inspired, would not be; why the errors?"

    - Answer: All of the historical pertinent data must be available to prove a true contradiction.
        1) And the testimony of Scripture must be correctly represented.
        2) So far, many so-called contradictions have been resolved by further archeological evidence.
        3) A contradiction exists, not when two statements differ, but only when both cannot possibly be true.

4. Objection: "Do not some biblical writers actually disclaim inspiration" (i.e. Paul in I Corinthians 7:10, 12, 25)?

    - Answer: When those alleged disclaimers are examined, they vanish!
        1) To the contrary, Paul merely states that the Lord had not spoken specifically on these themes.

2) The apostles were guided into all truth (John 16:13).
3) Even when Paul stated his opinion (i.e., I Corinthians 7:25), he was also stating that his opinion in this case had the sanction of God.
4) Paul was not a whit behind any of the other apostles (II Corinthians 11:5).
5) That which the apostle taught was from the Lord (I Corinthians 14:37).
6) Hence he could both "charge" and "ordain" with authority from God (I Corinthians 7:10, 17, 40).

The Case For Absolute Authority

The assertion that the concepts or ideas of Scripture are inspired, but not the words, is how modernists are able to explain away passages of Scripture as they please, denying the verbal inspiration of the Bible.

This type of interpretation lends itself to the subjective basis of understanding. Who is right when the person says that it feels right or the person says the Bible says it is right? If the Bible cannot be trusted as reliable, then there is no ABSOLUTE authority to go by in our everyday decisions in regards to moral and ethical problems.

The verbal (word for word) inspiration of the Bible requires an objective basis for interpretation using the meaning of the "words" as final authority. What good are "infallible ideas" if they are channeled through "fallible words?" As the Apostle Paul said, "Let God be true, and every man a liar. As it is written: 'So that you [God] may be proved right when you speak and prevail when you judge'" (Romans 3:4; Psalm 51:4).

The Bible came from God. Otherwise there is no way to explain its continuity over sixteen hundred years by over forty writers. How else can you explain its superior moral and ethical codes as are found in the Ten Commandments and the Sermon on the Mount? The Bible is trustworthy and will make us wise unto salvation. The biblical counselor can feel confident in the Bible as a standard that is true, objective and divine.

Review Questions

1. How does the "Dead Sea Scrolls" prove the accuracy of the Bible?
2. What are the two requirements for a so-called contradiction to exist?
3. How would you define "Plenary Verbal Inspiration?"
4. What does II Timothy 3:16, 17 prove about inspiration?
5. What did Peter mean when he said, "no prophecy of Scripture is a matter of one's own interpretation?"
6. What is the definition of the Greek word "theopneustos?"
7. What does the story of king Belshazzar of Babylon prove about the reliability of the Bible?
8. Who were the Hittites?

Chapter Nine

THE DESIGN AND ORDER OF GOD'S CREATION

"In the beginning God created the heavens and the earth" (Genesis 1:1). When the biblical account of creation is taken literally, not mystically or parabolically, every known fact of science or history can be conveniently and correctly placed within the biblical framework (Isaiah 40:12, 22).

As to the nature of God's creative work, the following things should be emphasized:

1. All was created perfect and full-grown (Genesis 1:1-26).
2. All creation was completed in six twenty-four hour days.
3. All creation was non-evolutionary (in terms of transcending "kinds" as a classification).
4. All creation was created out of things not seen (Hebrews 11:3).

Which came first – the chicken or the egg? Evolutionists cannot give an answer to this question. They cannot conceive of an egg coming into being without a chicken nor a chicken without an egg being hatched. The Bible believer has no problem with this. Man has never created anything. He has produced life from live tissue in a "test tube," in a "petri dish" or in the "womb," but he has never created life out of nothing. Only God has done that.

There is nothing in the Genesis account of creation that contradicts any known fact of science. Six times in the first chapter of Genesis the record says that God evaluated His handiwork as "good" (Genesis 1:4, 10, 12, 18, 21, 25). There was no disorder or "struggle for survival" involved in the bringing about of our world and its inhabitants.

All things were created in perfect harmony and order. In the theory of evolution, all things are said to be going from a SIMPLER to a more COMPLEX state of being, from a more "disordered" arrangement to a more "orderly" one. The biblical account makes the process work in the exact reverse. The long lives of the Patriarchs due to climatic conditions are an example of this.

In his book, Charles Darwin contended that natural selection is the "mechanism" of evolution that brings about survival of the fittest, and that all of life originated from one single cell source.[37] The Bible claims a "finished" creation – not a continuing process, which is constantly producing new forms (Hebrews 4:3).

The Genesis account affirms that the basic forms of biological life were created "after their kind" (Genesis 1:11-25). The word "kind" (Hebrew word is "min") is a generic term that is broader than what scientists commonly designate as a "species." For example, the owl is classified as a "kind" and yet there are more than 250 known species of owl (Leviticus 11:16-18). There is room, therefore, within the biblical group called "kind" for horizontal variation. This does not, however, allow for the vertical evolution that is essential to the Darwinian theory, i.e., the notion that all of earth's creatures have resulted from a solitary primitive organism. In the "evolutionary model," the universe is self-contained and has come into being through mechanistic processes without any kind of supernatural intervention.

The Law of Biogenesis

The evidence of the Law of Biogenesis (cause and effect) shows there are no uncaused things. The inanimate – the sun, moon, stars and earth imply a cause. Reason rejects the idea that a house happened without a cause (Hebrews 3:4). "Spontaneous generation" is one of the fundamental concepts of evolution. Dr. George Wald of Harvard has stated: "The reasonable view was to believe in spontaneous generation; the only alternative, is to believe in a single, primary act of supernatural creation. There is no third alternative."[38] Evolutionists concur that spontaneous generation is not now occurring. But what evidence do we have that it ever did occur?

Evolution (spontaneous generation) demands a creation of all living things from a single cell that somehow was developed through some combustion of gases in the universe. The Law of Biogenesis states that all life comes from preceding life and that of its kind. Dr. Bert Thompson states, "neither in nature nor in the laboratory have we documented a single case of spontaneous generation."[39]

The creation model predicts, like the Law of Biogenesis (which is a reality in nature), that life comes only from preceding life, and that of its kind.

Evolution predicts exactly the opposite and makes its prediction on a total lack of evidence. While evolution is making its case on evidence, which is admittedly not available, the case for creation is based upon scientific evidence, which is available – the Law of Biogenesis. "The case for creation, however, is not based in imagination. Creation is based instead on logical inference from our scientific observation."[40]

The universe shows evidence, not only of being made but also of having been arranged (Hebrews 3:4). It is a COSMOS not a CHAOS. A can of alphabet soup implies a maker, but a poem implies not only a maker but also an intelligent arranger.

If design is present, a "Designer" must exist (Romans 1:18-20). Such is human logic and if we cannot depend on human logic, how can the evolutionist demand we believe in his logic? If we take the argument of "simplicity," the Law of Parsimony, we conclude that the simplest solution to a problem is better than the complex.

What is the cause of the universe? Where did order come from? Where did design come from? What is the meaning of life? Where did the desire for immortality come from? A belief in a moral God can explain all of this. Evolution and atheism cannot explain any of this in a simplistic way. Charles Darwin said that the argument of design was the hardest to overcome in proving the evolutionary theory. He called it "an utterly hopeless muddle."

The Law of Photosynthesis argues for a designer. This is the process of the biological synthesis of chemical compounds in the presence of light. The process by which plant cells make carbohydrates from carbon dioxide (exhaled by all animals) and water in the presence of chlorophyll and light, and release oxygen as a by-product. This process produces oxygen for all living things. Such a process requires a design for human life, plant life, animal life, sun radiation, etc., and all are interrelated and interdependent. Such a process requires a DESIGNER.

The Big Bang Theory

The Big Bang Theory alleges that some 20 billion years ago (give or take a billion) all of the matter in the known universe was tightly packed into a microscopic cosmic "egg." One writer expresses it this way: "Astonishingly, scientists now calculate that everything in this vast universe grew out of a region many billions of times smaller than a single proton, one of the atom's basic particles."[41]

In one of his books, Dr. Robert Jastrow asserts that in the beginning "all matter in the universe was compressed into an infinitely dense and hot mass" that exploded. Over many eons, supposedly, "the primordial cloud of the universe expands and cools, stars are born and die, the sun and earth are formed, and life arises on the earth."[42] This assumes that "matter" is eternal. But this idea is refuted by our knowledge of physics (e.g., the Second Law of Thermodynamics). None of these materialistic theories has any credibility – biblically or scientifically.

The Big Bang Theory speculates that the marvelously ordered universe randomly resulted from a gigantic explosion. Explosions have been known to destroy life, not create it. The immensity of the problem of first getting inorganic to give rise to organic, and then non-living to give rise to living is not only impossible to imagine it has not been proven scientifically.

Drs. Green and Goldberger have stated, "There is one step [in evolution] that far outweighs the others in enormity; the step from macromolecules to cells. All other steps can be accounted for on theoretical grounds – if not correctly, at least elegantly. However, the macromolecule to cell transition is a jump of fantastic dimensions, which lies beyond the range of testable hypothesis. In this area, all is conjecture. The available facts do not provide a basis for postulation that cells arose on this planet."[43]

Evolutionary theories require a primitive Earth with conditions that allow the chemical reactions, which are believed to have been involved in processes leading to the origin of life. If the early Earth contained free oxygen, biochemical evolution would have been completely impossible.

As one scientist points out, "As soon as the conditions become oxidizing [caused by oxygen in the atmosphere], the organic syntheses will effectively turn off. None of the essential molecules of life, e.g. amino acids, could even be formed under oxidizing conditions, and if by some chance they were, they would decompose quickly. Chemical evolution would be impossible."[44] It is also a scientific fact that, "...water in any case inhibits the growth of more complex molecules." (Francis Hitching)

There must have been oxygen in the atmosphere when the Earth was brought into being, because without oxygen, there is no ozone canopy to protect Earth from the sun's destructive ultraviolet rays.

Dr. Thaxton goes on to say, "But it is a scientific fact that organic compounds (such as the essential precursor chemicals or basic building blocks that must have accumulated for chemical evolution to proceed) are decomposed rather quickly in the presence of oxygen."[45]

Science cannot support the theory of "spontaneous generation." In the real world, every effect must have an adequate cause. But in the strange land of evolutionary incredulity, wonderful things can "just happen!"

Instead of the world becoming more complex, it is becoming less energy efficient and it is winding down. While things quantitatively remain stable, they qualitatively deteriorate. In all energy transformations, there is a tendency for some of the energy to be transformed into non-reversible heat energy. This is called the Second Law of Thermodynamics (Hebrews 1:10-12).

The First Law of Thermodynamics says nothing is being created at this time and that energy can be transformed in various ways, but it cannot be destroyed. Everything we have is a result of energy.

The Second Law of Thermodynamics reveals that the universe is winding down. A log has energy. There are molecules moving within it. If you burn a log, you are using the log's energy. When you finish with the burning, you have ashes remaining, which are chemicals, and in which molecules are moving, so you still have energy but it has diminished in its usefulness.

When you then add the energy of the heat to the energy of the ashes, you will have the total that was in the log. You have not destroyed the energy, but you have "transformed" it from one source to another and it is less usable.

The evolutionary theory says that everything is moving from the simple to the complex. This is the opposite of known and available scientific facts.

There Are No Observable Facts To Support Evolution

Charles Darwin did not form his evolutionary views because he discovered scientific facts that indicate that evolution had occurred. He was a ministerial student in Cambridge University in the late 1820's (evolutionary theories pre-date Darwin by about 2400 years). He turned away from the Bible because he thought it contained contradictions. He then formed his evolutionary views, not because of scientific evidences, but he said he did so because he did not want to believe in "nothing."

Darwin thought the fossil record in the earth's crust would support his evolutionary doctrine, but he was not able to prove the fossil record supported his views. This became a monumental flaw in his theory.

The Fossil Record reveals no transitional forms of life. "The earliest and most primitive known members [mammals] of every order already have the basic ordinal characters and in no case is an approximately continuous sequence from one order to another known."[46] (George Gaylord Simpson, an evolutionary paleontologist) Simpson goes on to say, "In most cases the break is so sharp and the gap so large that the origin of the order is speculative and much disputed. This regular absence of transitional forms is not confined to mammals, but is an almost universal phenomenon, as has long been noted by paleontologists. It is true of almost all orders of all classes of animals, both vertebrate and invertebrate. It is also true of analogous categories of plants."[47] The fossil record reveals that there are no transitional forms of life transcending from one kind to another.

The biblical record tells us that all life was created at one time. The fossil record assuredly does not indicate that all forms of life have evolved from an original primitive source (or even a few sources).

Dr. Duane T. Gish, in his popular book states, "The abrupt appearance of a great variety of highly complex forms of life and sudden appearance of the higher categories of plants and animals with no evidence of transitional forms between these basic kinds, provide excellent support for special creation, but contradict the major predictions of evolutionary theory."[48]

The Anthropic Principle

The term "anthropic" derives from the Greek word "anthropos," which is the generic term for mankind. The expression suggests that the universe in general, and our solar system in particular, appears to have been specially designed for human existence.[49] Only a supreme being could have created such a system.

The facts point to a universal God, who made the universe. Our own galaxy, the Milky Way, is over 100,000 light years in diameter. However, this universe in which we live is composed of 2.5 million other galaxies comparable to the Milky Way.[50]

The Sun, which heats our galaxy's system, is poised at 93 million miles from the Earth. If it were just ten percent closer, it would literally burn everything to a crisp. If it were just ten percent farther away, we would be frozen solid in a matter of minutes due to the extreme cold. The Moon, which is poised in space at 240,000 miles from the Earth, would cause 35 to

50 feet tides over the entire Earth twice a day if it were moved just one-fifth closer.

The Earth is traveling through space around the Sun at a speed of 70,000 miles per hour or 19 miles a second.

The Solar system itself is traveling through space at a speed of over 600,000 miles per hour. The Solar system takes an estimated 220 million years just to complete an orbit. If the Earth traveled at only 35,000 miles per hour, just one-half of its current rate, our seasons would be doubled, and the intense summer heat would bake the Earth while the intense winter cold would freeze it.

The Earth's axis is inclined from the perpendicular to the plain of its orbit by twenty-three and one-half degrees. This tilt of the Earth accounts for the seasons. If it were not tilted, the water vapor from the ocean would move north and south, piling up continents of ice and leaving possibly a desert between the equator and the ice. The weight of the unbelievably vast mass of ice would depress the poles, causing our equator to bulge or erupt or at least show the need of a new waistline. Wrapped around our earth is a protective blanket that we call atmosphere. It is composed mainly of nitrogen (78%), oxygen (21%), and carbon dioxide (0.03%), along with water vapor and minute levels of several other gases.[51]

The proper balance of these elements is absolutely essential to life on earth. Someone mixed them just RIGHT! Who do you suppose that Someone is? I don't believe it happened accidentally.

The Six Days of Creation

The matter of whether or not the Bible says that these were six literal days can be settled primarily with one verse (evolution requires billions of years to develop). "For in six days the Lord made the heavens and earth, the sea, and all that is in them, but he rested on the seventh day" (Exodus 20:11; 31:16, 17). If everything was made in six twenty-four hour days, then nothing was made prior to or after (Genesis 1:1-31).

The Hebrew word for "days" in this verse is "yamin," in the plural form, and when in the plural form it normally refers to a literal 24-hour day. The most natural interpretation would be literal days. Words should be defined in the Bible literally unless the context demands otherwise (Genesis 2:1-4; 5:1-5).

In Exodus 20:11, the days are viewed as literal twenty-four hour days. The Hebrew word for "day" in Genesis One is "yom." When this word is associated with a "definite numeral," it is (unless the context indicates otherwise) a solar 24-hour day.

Each of the days of creation had an EVENING and a MORNING. How could the "evenings" and "mornings" have been days of millions of years each in the first chapter of Genesis? If such were the case, how would the vegetation have survived? It took God six days to create the world, because He intended six days of work and one day of rest to be a pattern for man to live by. After all, if He is God, could he not create the world in six minutes?

The Need For a Standard

To the Skilled Helper, the Bible must be the word of God and God must be who the Bible says He is. Much of psychological counseling today is based on the whims and opinions of so-called professionals. Who is right when it comes to theories of counseling or methodology? If there is no absolute authority, no God, no revelation from God that can be reliable, one opinion is as good as another and no psychological statement can be determined as absolute fact. If the universe was not created by God, then who gave it design and order? Without God, there is no such thing as a psychological law.

Dr. Lawrence Crabb sums it up in this statement: "Selecting a basic position on the nature of man, the universal so badly needed in the field of counseling, resembles a random throw at the dart board unless some objective source of knowledge is available."[52]

The Skilled Helper has an objective source of knowledge of humankind and all its weaknesses and needs and it is called the Bible, God's revelation to us. He/she can have a sense of competence, assurance, and absolute authority in the Scriptures.

Review Questions

1. What is the "Law of Biogenesis?"
2. What is the "Big Bang Theory?"
3. What is the "Second Law of Thermodynamics" and how does it refute evolution?
4. What is the "Anthropic Principle?"
5. How does the "Six Twenty-four Hour Days" prove special creation?
6. Why is an absolute standard needed in counseling psychology?
7. What is the "First Law of Thermodynamics?"
8. What are the four things that should be emphasized of the nature of God's creation?

Chapter Ten

REVIEW OF POPULAR COUNSELING THEORIES

This chapter is designed to introduce the biblical counselor to the basic concepts and theories of counseling and to examine the role that Christian principles play in the counseling process. The modern day counselor has many theories and methodologies to choose from in his training and preparation as a therapist.

Whether a professional or a non-professional, all counselors chose some kind of philosophy to guide them in their pursuit of helping people cope with personal problems. It is not just the counseling theory that we need to look at, but the underlying philosophy of man's origin and purpose in life. We will choose a method of therapy that coincides with our view of man and his place in the role of living things.

THEORIES BASED ON THE EVOLUTIONARY MODEL

The following are theories based on the assumption that man, and all forms of life, have been produced from one single life form billions of years ago. This hypothesis claims that man was not created (by a supreme being) and that he has no soul. It proclaims that man is just another animal, who happens to be on a higher plane of development due to the evolutionary forces of "natural selection." If a counselor has such a belief system about man's origin, it will affect his method of therapy and his concept of morality.

The Psychodynamic Theory

No psychologist has had more influence on modern day psychology and psychiatry than Sigmund Freud. He was born in 1856 in Austria and he died in 1939. Freud has had a radical impact on the theories of human nature.

His theories about human behavior have permeated all of society. He is the most quoted and respected therapist in the world. He has been credited with being the one who lifted psychiatry from the backrooms of palm readers and soothsayers to the mainstream of intellectuals and respected society.

Through Freud's efforts, psychology has reached a status in our society as a science in and of itself. Yet, today many therapists do not accept his conclusions on human nature. This being said, he is still believed to be, by the common man, the standard by which psychiatry is judged.

Sigmund Freud's psychoanalysis focuses on three themes:

1. Emphasis on "sex" and "aggression" as a motivational basis for behavior.
2. A focus on "deterministic" and "naturalistic" assumptions of the psychodynamic model.
3. The "direct attack" on religion that Freud made in his later writings.

Classic "psychoanalysis" assumes that all human behavior is determined by "psychic" energy and early childhood experiences. In order to make sense of a person's current behavior patterns, it is necessary to understand the behavior's roots in largely unconscious conflicts and motives. The forces, according to Freud, that move us are irrational and strong, and most often are related to aggressive or sexual impulses. He believed we are basically animals and therefore, all motives are instinctually based.

Freud was influenced heavily by Julian Huxley's defense of the evolutionary theories of Charles Darwin. Thus, he became convinced that man was just an animal of a higher intelligence than other animals. His theories on human behavior were more or less based on evolution.

His structural assumptions assert that the psychic apparatus can best be understood in terms of three separate but interdependent entities known as the "id," the "ego," and the "superego." The "id" is the entity where our most primitive sexual and aggressive drives and urges are. "Id" processes are assumed to be present at birth and largely unconscious, illogical, demanding and relentlessly driving toward personal gratification. The "ego" is reality-based and develops as an individual interacts with the external world. The "ego" is largely conscious and serves a vital role in mediating the primitive urges of the "id" with constraints or opportunities of reality. The "superego" places restrictive demands on both the "id" and the "ego." Often seen as a kind of "conscience," the "superego" is assumed to be only partially conscious.

The Freudian development of personality is a series of psychosexual stages:

1. The "oral stage" (first year of life). It focuses on the gratification (or lack thereof) as a baby on the mouth: sucking and chewing.
    a. Failure to get one's needs met potentially leads to greediness and an unhealthy preoccupation with possessions later in life.
2. The "anal stage" (ages 1 to 3) centers around the child's experience of parental demands, discipline and expectations, especially as they relate to toilet training. Unresolved issues (psychic gratification centers on retention or expulsion) lead to unhealthy attitudes about bodily functions.
3. The "phallic stage" (ages 3 to 6) focuses on gratification of the genitals. Unresolved issues distort sexuality later in life.
4. The "latency stage" (ages 6-12) emphasizes increased socialization with other children and directly relates to academic, athletic, interpersonal or recreational competencies, which impact self-concepts.
5. The "genital stage" (ages 12-18) is where again sexual impulses become predominant. Healthy or unhealthy interest in the opposite sex develops in this stage.

The ultimate goal of psychoanalysis is the total reconstruction of the basic personality. In order to accomplish this goal, it is necessary to relive certain painful childhood experiences and work through them. This process is called "abreaction" or "catharsis."

In the psychoanalytic tradition, healthy individuals are ones who have enough conscious awareness of their basic issues to have self-control. Earlier painful and traumatic experiences have largely been "worked through" and are no longer denied or distorted. To a meaningful degree and significant degree, aspects of the unconscious have been made conscious. Important dimensions of the personality structure have been reconstructed, as neurotic processes have been undone, thereby facilitating greater movement toward maturity.

There are certain conclusions in Freud's theories that have some merit in counseling, but much of what he wrote is based in the philosophy that man is just an animal. As such, man should therefore be looked upon as just another living being, basically controlled by animal instincts. Freud has based his philosophy of therapy on these conclusions.

The Behavioral Theory

The Behavioral Theory of counseling was first given clear articulation by the famous John B. Watson (1920's). He promoted the concept of "naturalism." Naturalism assumes that the universe is composed exclusively of matter and energy hence there are no such things as "supernatural" entities such as gods or spirits. The specific formula for understanding behavior was supplied later by the learning theories of Pavlov, Thorndike, B.F. Skinner and others.

In Behaviorism, all human and animal behavior is viewed as caused by events in the environment. Behavioral understandings of the person are generally that the person is a bundle of behavior patterns, reflexes, perceptions and impressions.

The self is nothing more than the aggregation of the person's empirical characteristics. In behavioral assessment, it is not persons or personalities that are assessed, but behaviors and the controlling variables. The committed behaviorist asserts that "classical" and "operant" learning processes explain man's behavior. The following is a breakdown of such:

1. "Operant learning" is also called instrumental learning. It refers to the modification of freely emitted behavior; that is, behavior which is free in the sense of being non-reflexive and non-coerced.
2. "Classical conditioning" is the process by which an involuntary response becomes reflexively associated with new eliciting stimuli. All human beings exhibit reflexive responses that are unlearned (or unconditioned) to stimuli that elicit these responses from us, as when the smell of food elicits salivation, a puff of air elicits eye blinking, a burn elicits pain, a noxious odor elicits nausea and so forth.

      a. The classic example is Pavlov's dogs, which learned to salivate at the sound of a bell, because of the repeated association of the bell with the presentation of food.
      b. In this case, the food was the "unconditioned stimulus," which elicited an "unconditioned response" of salivation.
      c. After the conditioning trials, the previously irrelevant bell became a "conditioning stimulus."
3. "Operant conditioning" is different in the sense that an emitted behavior is modified over time by the consequences that follow contingent upon the responses and by the stimuli that form the context under which the behavior occurs.

Behaviorism's embrace of naturalism gave rise to what has been called "reductionism," the principle of breaking down more complex phenomena into simpler, more elemental ones. Thus human language became understood as "verbal behavior," operating on the same principles as all overt behavior and reflexes.

Another implication of naturalism was "environmentalism," not in the ecological sense but in the sense that all behaviors are caused by factors outside of or external to themselves. All human and animal behavior is viewed as caused by events in the environment. If the behaviors of human beings are merely a part of the stream of natural, material events occurring in a mechanistic cosmos, then it surely follows that all our actions, including even what we call our decisions and choices, are caused in such a way that, we always do what we must do. Human choice is ultimately illusory; our actions are the inevitable results of the causal forces impinging on us.

There is much to accept in the Behavioral Therapy methodology that helps the counselor to realize that we are, to a degree, programmed in our thinking to respond to stimuli in certain ways as a result of a conditioning process. This truth has helped social scientists in many ways to understand human behavior.

But in emphasizing only bodily existence, the behaviorist misses a key aspect of human nature, that being the existence of the soul and the spirit and the transcending nature of man in seeking and longing for a higher power (Acts 17:24-28).

This theory ignores the ability of man to project beyond his current situation and to make adjustments in his status, not by instinct or conditioning, but by an inherent moral compass (Romans 2:14-16).

The Non-Directive Theory

Probably no theory of counseling and psychotherapy more fully manifests the humanistic spirit in contemporary psychology than does Non-Directive Therapy (often called Person-Centered Therapy), and perhaps no single individual better embodied its essence than its founder, Carl Rogers.

The Non-Directive theory is an ever-evolving approach since the early 1940's; it has experienced a noticeable renewal in the latter part of the Twentieth Century. It boldly asserts that the client, not the therapist, should be at the heart of the counseling method since only the counselee has the resources by which to become more aware of and able to remove his/her obstacles to personal growth.

Perhaps the core assertion of this personality theory is that there is but one motivational force for all humanity: the tendency toward "self-actualization." All persons have an inherent tendency to develop their capacities to the fullest, in ways that will either maintain or enhance their own well-being.

It is significant that Rogers preaches a theory that subscribes to the belief there is no absolute authority. Rogers believed that each person's perception of who he is and who he can be, leads to healing without direction from the therapist. The therapist is not allowed to impose any moral judgments or any standard of truth on the counselee.

Thus, Non-Directive means that the therapist does not direct the counselee, only guides him through repeating the counselee's statements for clarification, hoping the counselee will see the error of his ways and make the proper correction.

It is quite clear that this therapy is a reaction against what Rogers perceived as the dogmatism of "prescriptive" religion. It certainly is a reaction against the authority of the God of the Bible, and leaves the counselee helpless and hopeless.

THEORIES BASED ON THE BIBLICAL MODEL

The following counseling theories are based on the belief that man is a distinct being, capable, to a degree, of determining his own destiny and accepting an absolute standard of authority. The basis for that authority must be a supreme being. To the Christian it is the God of the Bible.

These theories may not be spoken of in the Bible, but they are based on the principle in the Bible that all men/women are created by God and are to be responsible for their decisions and the consequences that come from those decisions.

The Cognitive Theory

The term "cognitive" comes from the word "cognition" and it means, "the process of knowing in the broadest sense, including perception, memory, judgment, etc."[53] It is a therapy that looks to the mind (and its thought processes) as the main motivator of human behavior.

The main contributors to this therapy process are Albert Ellis (1962) and A.T. Beck (1979). Although neither man is recognized as a Christian, and neither looked to the Bible as a final authority, the results of their research developed into a methodology that, in most aspects, uniquely coincides with the biblical model and mandate for human behavior.

The Bible requires believers to not be conformed to this world, but be transformed by the renewing (changing belief systems) of the mind (Romans 12:2).

Cognitive therapy typically proceeds in three stages:

1. The presentation of the cognitive theory.
2. The development of an awareness of the dysfunctional thoughts on the part of the counselee.
3. The changing of thoughts and the substitution of more functional thinking.

Christian scholars, who have given a more biblical emphasis to this theory, are: William Backus, Ph.D. (Telling Yourself The Truth) and Chris Thurman, Ph.D. (The Lies We Believe). Therefore, this theory has a biblical orientation as opposed to the humanistic theories of Freud, Skinner and Rogers. The basis of this theory is that man can change his feelings and behavior through the process of rational thoughts. In fact, Ellis called this therapy "Rational Emotive Therapy" (RET).

The Temperament Theory

We now look at a theory that is becoming more and more accepted in Christian counseling circles. This theory is basic to the belief that, we are created by God with different temperaments. In fact, some counselors call this "Creation Therapy."

The "temperament" in simple terms, is the genetic, inborn part of man that determines how we react to people, places and things. It reveals certain characteristics and traits that are a part of us, and that reveal what we are. In short, it is how we interpret our environment and interact with it. The temperament pinpoints our perceptions of ourselves (and the people who love us). It is also the determining factor in how well we handle the stresses and pressures of today.

Hippocrates (460-370 B.C.) was the first to bring to light the theory of "temperament," even though he may have been building on the thoughts of Impedocles (495-435 B.C.). Since Hippocrates did not have the scientific tools that are available today, his theories were based on his observations of man's behavior. According to Hippocrates, man's behavior was governed by the color of bile within a person's body.

The body fluids, which Hippocrates called "humors," were divided into four classifications: 1. Blood, 2. Black Bile, 3. Yellow Bile, and 4. Phlegm. He believed that an excess of one or more of these fluids would cause the person to behave according to the nature of the fluid(s); i.e., a person who had an over-abundance of black bile would be an extremely dark, moody person, as in "melancholy." As we know today, the theory of "humors" has proven to be scientifically unsound, but it has given us a basic understanding of the differences in human behavior.

In 1927, Alfred Adler interpreted Hippocrates' four temperaments as the "Sanguine," "Choleric," "Melancholic," and "Phlegmatic."

Dr. Tim LaHaye, a well known contemporary Christian author and psychologist, has successfully challenged the Christian community with the probability that "temperament" needs and traits are God-given characteristics, and are genetically inbred differences of uniqueness.[54]

Many temperament therapists believe that the "temperament" is who we really are (characteristics and traits unique to the person) and the "personality" is who we portray ourselves to be. The wider the difference between the temperament and personality, the higher the anxiety/stress level a person will experience. This produces a stronger possibility of engaging in destructive and compulsive/obsessive behavior.

This author is a Licensed Pastoral Counselor with the National Christian Counselor's Association, which endorses the Temperament Theory and has developed the "Temperament Analysis Profile." This profile reveals from the questions answered, the temperament traits and characteristics of the counselee. This profile is quite accurate, which I can attest to, having used it with over 150 clients as of the date of this writing.

The Nouthetic Theory

What is "Nouthetic Counseling?" The founder of Nouthetic Counseling is Jay Adams, who has written on the subject extensively.[55] Adams coined the phrase "nouthetic counseling" from a passage in the Bible. As we define the concept of nouthethic counseling, we must also define the word "nouthetic." The Greek words "nouthesis" and "noutheteo," are the noun and verb forms in the New Testament, from which he derives the term "nouthetic." The word is found in Romans 15:14 and Colossians 3:16. It is normally translated as: "admonish," "instruct" or "counsel." The word has the connotation of "confronting one another."

Nouthetic confrontation consists in at least three basic elements:

1. It implies that there is a problem.
2. It is confrontation with the intent of making a change in the counselee.
3. It is teaching with the purpose of influencing for good.

In Romans 15:14, the apostle Paul reveals that the Christian can counsel others and is qualified if he/she is full of "goodness" and "knowledge." It is training by the Word of God, and with the intent of correcting the problem and making it right before God (Galatians 6:1, 2).

It is "directive" counseling as opposed to "non-directive," which is the Rogerian approach. It is Christian counseling that involves the use of "authoritative" instruction. It depends on the Word of God as final authority, not the "end justifies the means; rather, it regulates the means."

Nouthetic counseling requires responsibility on the part of the counselor and counselee. It requires a desire on the part of the counselee to acknowledge sins and repent. It requires on the part of the counselee the willingness to accept the Bible as the final authority. It requires the counselee to face his/her problems and find a biblical solution.

There is much to commend in "nouthetic counseling," but the problem I see with the writings of Jay Adams is that he seems to spurn the idea that psychology has any merit as a therapy for the Christian. He also leaves me with the impression that the Bible and prayer can address all problems without the need for any psychological knowledge to draw from. I have already addressed the idea that psychology, if properly applied with biblical principles, is effective because it is a study of the mind that God made. I believe that the Nouthetic Theory is commendable but lacking in appreciation of true psychological laws that can help the counselor when dealing with hurting people.

The Misbelief Theory

"Misbelief Therapy," is a label that was originally coined by William Backus, a clinical psychologist. Backus writes, "Misbelief Therapy, as we have called our 'modus operandi,' involves putting the truth into our value systems, philosophies, demands, expectations, moralistic and emotional assumptions, as well as into the words we tell ourselves."[56]

The brain can be programmed to believe lies as well as truth. When the repetition of lies becomes consistent, the brain records them as truth and it can recall such belief systems at will, subconsciously. These lies work to destroy us and cause us to make wrong decisions and develop behavior that is self-destructive. The Misbelief Theory is built on the Cognitive Model of therapy with a total focus on the truth based in the Scriptures. It is the premise of this book, and the basis for "biblical counseling."

In Misbelief Therapy, the individual's cognitive processes are believed to be the primary cause of all feelings and behavior. Even the most bizarre disorders, the complete withdrawal of a person from reality, or the irrational thoughts of a mentally ill person are deeply meaningful and considered a result of faulty thinking in the counselee's belief systems in this theory. To the misbelief therapist, although the well-trained psychologist or psychiatrist may not understand every detail of the patient's symptoms, a process of evaluating the counselee's self-talk is a tested assumption with a belief that the symptoms of mental illness can be interpreted as a result of faulty thinking.

There are occasions when the inner stress and confusion felt by a person are sufficient to impair his day-to-day functioning. It is almost as if facing his everyday problems were too much for him and his self-talk is creating negative feelings and behavior. He then finds communicating with family and friends extremely difficult, functioning on his job is a heavy burden, and he tends to deny reality. The misbelief therapist will consider the possibility of a physical cause, but after this is eliminated as a cause, he will begin a series of counseling sessions defining the self-talk and seeking to help the counselee to remove the lies and replace them with the truth.

The primary basis for the Misbelief Theory is that environmental stress (or trauma) is not the primary cause of neurotic behavior, but the faulty interpretation of the counselee's environment causes the faulty thinking, which in turn creates the stress and trauma.

We believe that Misbelief Therapy is a biblical model based on the biblical principle of the apostle Paul's admonition when he says, "Do not conform any longer to the pattern of this world, but be transformed by the renewing of your mind" (Romans 12:2). Changing the mind and its belief systems is the essence of Misbelief Theory and the foundation of biblical conversion to the Lord Jesus Christ.

Review Questions

1. How would you describe the "Psychodynamic Theory?"
2. What is the major flaw in the "Behavioral Theory?"
3. What are the three stages of "Cognitive Therapy?"
4. What are the three basic elements in the "Nouthetic Theory?"
5. What is the difference between "Temperament" and "Personality?"
6. How would you define "environmentalism?"
7. What is the significance of Pavlov's dogs?
8. How would you define "operant conditioning?"

Chapter Eleven

THE BIBLE AND CHRISTIAN ETHICS

In our world today, the concept of "ethics" is determined by the situation one is in. "Situation ethics" is the moderate approach between the two extremes of "legalism" (saved by law-keeping) and "antinomianism" (no absolute moral law). It contends that all written codes of law are not really "laws" in the sense of being permanent and unchangeable. They are only guidelines or general principles that may or may not reveal the right and loving response for a given situation.

"The situationist enters into every decision-making situation fully armed with ethical maxims of his community and its heritage, and he treats them with respect as illuminators of his problems. Just the same he is prepared in any situation to compromise them or set them aside in the situation, if love seems better served by doing so."[57]

Thus, what is "right" may differ in any given situation depending on what the "loving" response is. The highest moral principle is indeed (agape) love. Agape love is "unconditional love" and has the intent of doing what is best for another. It is at once the intent of all law and the summation or fulfillment of all revealed commands. Love is the guiding and motivating force behind all Christian thought, speech and behavior (Romans 13:8-10). But love requires of us that we keep the commandments of God (John 14:15).

ABORTION

Abortion, as such, is not in the Bible. There is a reference to a miscarriage, and it does give us an idea of God's will, in regards to the sanctity of life (Exodus 21:22-25). The question is, "When does the 'embryo' become a living viable organism, or when does this developing 'fetus' have a soul" (Psalm 139:13-16)? I believe it happens at the point of conception.

When we look at the science of embryology and try to leave the emotions out of the debate, we find that the truth is that at the point of conception there is a completely new human being coming into the world. Whatever human rights we may have do not allow us to destroy a human life. Our bodies do not belong to us (I Corinthians 6:19, 20).

A Look at Embryology

A. At conception life begins:

1. All that we are – height, hair and eye color, sex – is included in the single cell called a "zygote."
2. Day 2: The zygote splits into two cells, then splits again and again into a bundle of cells called a "blastocyst."
3. Week 1: As a bundle of cells, we implant ourselves in our mother's uterine wall.
4. By 3 weeks: The structure of all our basic organs and our fundamental body shape are beginning to be put in place, from brain to simple fingers.
5. By 4 weeks: We have a discernible heartbeat.
6. By 6 weeks: Our brain reveals electrical impulses.
7. By 7 weeks: Our neural cells in the brain begin to connect, and we begin to move spontaneously.
8. By 8 weeks: We're around 1 ½ inches long, and have all our organs.
   - Our hands, feet and limbs are clearly shaped.
   - Even our brain has convoluted folds, like that of an adult's.
   - Every minute about 100,000 nerve cells begin to sprout until there are around one billion at our birth.
   - At this point we are called a "fetus."
9. By 8 to 9 weeks: Ultrasound can pick up our fingerprints, footprints, even the creases in our palms.
10. By 10 weeks: We become very active – sucking our thumbs, jumping, scratching our head, and playing with our umbilical cord, our lifeline to our mother.
11. By 11 weeks: We are about three inches long and weigh one ounce.
    - We look and behave like the complete human beings we are.

- Our hearts are beating, our brains are active, and all bodily systems are working.
- We can suck our thumb, make a fist, hiccup, sleep, dream, hear, feel, urinate, and have tiny bowel movements.
- THIS IS THE AVERAGE AGE OF AN ABORTION!

12. By 12 weeks: We can grasp with our hands.
13. By 12-16 weeks: We'll move back if you touch our feet or body.
14. By 4 months: We can frown, move our lips, turn our head, kick our feet, and grasp with our hands. We even grow a little hair.
15. By 4 ½ months: We respond to a touch on our lips by sucking; just like a newborn baby.
16. By 6 months: Our nervous system is developed enough so that only the part of our body that's been touched will recoil from the touch.
17. By 7 months: We're in high gear. Our eyes can open and we respond to light. We also process and respond to sound – like the rush of blood through Mom's arteries.
    - In essence, our neural circuits are the way they'll be when we're newly born.
    - We can pay attention to speech directed to us through a loudspeaker, and repetitious sounds will bore us – our heartbeat will speed up, as if to drown out the boredom.
18. By 8 months: Our brain will have the same number of cells as we will have at birth.
19. By 9 months: Our cerebral cortex, the part of our brain associated with thought and consciousness, is well defined.
    - Our brain waves are similar to those we'll have as newborns: sleeping, dreaming, and waking.
    - We're ready to be born.
    - We decide the day of birth by signaling that labor contractions should begin.
20. WATCH OUT WORLD, HERE WE COME![58]

God's Interest in Human Development

God does take an interest in humans as they develop (Genesis 25:23; Job 31:15; 33:4-6; Psalm 139:13-16; Ecclesiastes 11:5; Isaiah 44:2, 24; 49:1-5). Even at an early age of development, God formed Jeremiah in the womb (Jeremiah 1:4, 5). Jesus was named before being conceived (Luke 2:21). The apostle Paul was called to be a preacher and set apart from his mother's womb (Galatians 1:15). John the Baptist leaped in Elizabeth's womb at six months at the voice of Mary (Luke 1:41).

Man is unique in God's creation. At some point of development God gives a baby a soul (Genesis 2:7, 19; Job 32:8). To destroy human life purposely, with intent, not in self-defense (and not for the purpose of saving another) is murder and the Bible does speak to that (Exodus 20:13; Deuteronomy 5:17; Matthew 5:21; 15:19; Romans 13:9; James 2:11). In 1974, the Supreme Court legalized abortion in the Roe v. Wade decision.

The Psychological Effect

The damage has been done! The immediate reaction after an abortion may be relief – no more fear of the unknown, but what about one month after the abortion, one year, or ten years. In-depth studies are reporting consistent findings. Psychological damage is taking the following forms:

- Guilt, anxiety, depression, a sense of loss, hostility, suicide, and psychosis are common consequences of abortion.
- And women suffer from not one but a combination of these difficulties.

Guilt over an abortion is a frequent reaction – a reaction that may smolder for years. Women confronting their guilt make such statements as, "I murdered my baby" or "I did something very wrong." Many fears can result from unresolved guilt, such as depression, self-accusation, phobias, or fears of infertility and of sex.

Anxiety and anger often are felt and expressed by women in the post-abortion period as well as anger towards those involved in the abortion. Women cry, "I'm going crazy" or "I'm always fearful." Many women are anxious about physical complications. Often worried that they may never have another child. In some cases there are no symptoms of physical problems, in others there are miscarriages or tubal pregnancies.

Women often describe symptoms of depression when telling of their feelings about their abortion experiences. Many feel completely immobilized. They haven't been interested in anyone or anything since their abortion. They don't talk to anyone, they don't go to work, and they don't function adequately in any area of life. In short, they are alienated from those around them and feel they have no one to confide in.

In their depression, many women find they have been crying since their abortions. They state, "I cry all the time." Others have insomnia and/or nightmares – nightmares about little boys or girls the age their children would have been. Some have constant, distressing flashbacks of the abortion procedure. During depressions (occurring frequently in the mid-decades of a patient's life) therapists frequently hear expressions of remorse and guilt concerning abortions that occurred twenty or more years earlier. Sometimes the patient's psychological pain from the abortion surfaces as they discuss another problem, the one that brought them to the therapist.

A family, who has experienced "amniocentesis" for the prenatal detection of an abnormality and has chosen abortion, is at risk of emotional trauma, also. Studies indicate that the incidence of depression following such selective abortion may be as high as 92 % among women, as high as 82% among men, and was greater than that associated with the delivery of a stillborn.[59] The cause of the pre-born baby's death makes the difference. A stillbirth usually is regarded as an unfortunate accident; while in a selective abortion, the baby's death is the result of a premeditated choice.

A sense of loss over the baby, who will never be, is articulated by women with reactions such as: "I cannot look at babies, little children, or pregnant women" or "I'm jealous of mothers," etc. There are always consequences from choices made outside the will of God. Premeditated abortion is a sin, but not unforgivable!

PORNOGRAPHY

The situation that we have in our cities is that pornography is everywhere, in the bookstands, the video shops and even on the Internet. This is a sin because it gives the impression that moral standards are no longer valid. It would be impossible to estimate the amount of influence that this sensuousness has had on the thinking of our young people with regard to sex and their relationships with one another. Pornography is a sin because it undermines the thinking and standards of all people and lowers us to the level of animals. Christians cannot afford to be involved in it in any way.

What is Pornography?

The word pornography comes from the Greek words PORNEIA meaning, "fornication; illicit sexual behavior" and GRAPHEI meaning, "writing" (I Corinthians 6:9-11). Thus pornography applies to illicit sexual behavior portrayed in the media – e.g., magazines, books, music, films, videos, sexual paraphernalia, the internet, etc. The apostle Paul condemns the activity of the Gentiles who had rejected God, by describing their activity as "being filled with all unrighteousness, sexual immorality (porneia), wickedness, covetousness and maliciousness" (Romans 1:29; NKJV).

Therefore, biblically, pornography can be defined as "media presentations, which implicitly or explicitly present language or action that is intended to, or tends to produce a sexual arousal in a person, which then creates illicit sexual thoughts and behavior" (some forms of dancing could be included in this category).

Although pornography directly applies only to sexual aberrations, it applies in principle to sexual violence, which is so prevalent in the media. In fact, studies show that pornography is the main catalyst that motivates sexual abusers.

The Government and Legal Issues

In 1983, congress passed legislation making child pornography illegal. In 1984, President Ronald Reagan called together a new Commission on Pornography. They found pornography, especially hard-core pornography, to be detrimental and degrading to society. Eighty percent of all hard-core pornography in the United States is produced in Los Angeles County.

In many respects the hands of our legislators and jurists are tied in matters involving ethics. One reason is because the current misinterpretation of the separation of church and state will not allow Congress to use religious standards of morality to judge obscenity. The world can never properly define or discriminate the obscene from that which is not because the world has no absolute criteria to make such a judgment.

The nature of God and the will of God emanating from His nature are the only criteria for absolute moral judgments. If one rejects God, there is no absolute standard by which to judge deviant behavior (Isaiah 55:7-9).

It all becomes a matter of personal taste, regardless of how repulsive one finds some actions to be. Majority rule does not determine right from wrong (Matthew 7:13, 14). All decisions based on personal taste are destined to cause confusion, contradiction, and legal gymnastics when it comes to defining pornography.

Pornography is Harmful

Pornography is degrading to people because it treats people as objects. It doesn't build integrity in persons made in God's image. It is harmful because it, and the fantasies that accompany it (including masturbation), creates a lust for illicit sex (Matthew 5:27-30). It is harmful because it is linked to violence in many forms.

Pornography has a correlation to rape, wife abuse, murder, and other felonies. Many sex abusers have testified to the fact that they fed their lust on pornography (e.g., Ted Bundy).

Lust is a sin against man and God. Pornography harms the family. Like other sins, pornography is addictive and progressive (James 1:13-15). Pornography is a sin, and a crime that our nation can do without.

MATERIALISM

A "materialistic" outlook causes a person to be primarily, if not exclusively, concerned with physical or material things and possessions, and is anti-Christian (Matthew 6:19-24). A typical dictionary definition of materialism would note the underlying professed belief or doctrine, which regards physical, material, empirical things as the only reality one can truly know. The consequence of this doctrine obliges its holder to maintain that everything in the world, including thought, will, and feeling, can be explained only in terms of material things.

In matters of personal conduct and motivation, the result of accepting this materialistic view of the nature of things is that one comes to embrace the view that comfort, pleasure, and wealth are the only real and highest goals and values. This general concept of materialism is powerful and effective in our world, and a compelling temptation to the Christian to allow such a view to overwhelm the spiritual values of his/her faith.

The Dangers of Materialism

The pervasiveness of the general danger of materialism is evident and the pull or tug on the Christian is real. Materialism can choke the spirituality from the heart (Luke 8:14). The danger of a person choking on food, the terror of someone being smothered in a plastic bag, the desperate rasping of a blocked air passage caused by a sharp blow are some examples. How much more the fright of the choking of the spirituality of a Christian, who allows material possessions, values, and concerns to stifle, slowly but surely, the very life of the soul.

Materialism can prevent Christian maturity (Philippians 3:7-11). How sad to note a fine Christian who begins well in God's service but becomes entangled with material things. The cares, riches, and pleasures of this life are the "stuff" which lure one into materialism. Materialism can keep us from being transformed from the world and its values to Christ as our Savior (Romans 12:1, 2). Christians have found themselves, who set out to obtain material goods and thought they could or would not be tempted, to have been overcome by such.

Materialism is a weapon of Satan (Ephesians 6:10-18). This battle is ongoing and is in the spiritual realm, where Satan is trying to control our mind (Colossians 3:1-3). Materialism must not control our lives, because we are not of this world; our citizenship is in heaven (Philippians 3:17-21). It is not to set the pattern or standard for our conduct. We must realize that covetousness, which is, "wantonness, absence of restraint, lustful desires and indecency," is idolatry (Colossians 3:5).

We must learn to be content in this life with what we have. Contentment does not mean complacency! God knows us personally and our struggles (Matthew 6:25-34). Paul "learned" how to be content (Philippians 4:11). Jesus tells us to put our trust in the Father, not this world. Peter tells us that God really does care about us (I Peter 5:7).

There is the danger of falling into temptations, snares, and lusts. Paul noted that godliness with contentment is great gain and observed that with food and clothing one should be content. Contentment is not based on circumstances. We must realize the awful result of materialism (I Timothy 6:6-10). The thought is that an individual, who impales himself on a stake or a sword, experiences the consequent pain. The metaphor of being pierced by a sword, whether it was set in defense or fallen on by accident, illustrates how the individual has now come to be injured severely. The vividness of the figure calls to mind that what was confidently denied in the beginning, has now become embedded in our inner being with spiritual anguish being the result.

We must see the goal in life as Paul did. The crown of life in heaven is greater by far than any riches or reward in this life (II Timothy 4:6-8). These insights from Scripture vividly make clear the dangers and pitfalls evident in this world that would steer us away from Christ.

HUMANISM

The dictionary defines humanism as, "The quality of being human; human nature; any system of thought or action based on the nature, dignity, interests, and ideals of man; or a modern, non-theistic, rationalistic movement that holds that man is capable of self-fulfillment, ethical conduct, etc., without recourse to super-naturalism."[60]

Humanists may have an interest in the humanities – and doubtless many of them do – but humanism does not mean devotion to the study of the humanities. "Humanities" refers to the study of classical art, architecture and literature. "Humanism" is an attitude of worldly values, a conviction that man is capable of determining his destiny, and that there is no absolute truth, and man is a law unto himself (Judges 21:24, 25).

Humanism and Atheism Go Together

According to the New World Dictionary's definition of humanism, the humanist rejects the supernatural (Jeremiah 10:23). Humanist Manifestos I and II leave no doubt about the humanists' denial of God's existence. It says, "We find insufficient evidence for belief in the existence of a supernatural... As non-theists we begin with humans not God, nature not deity."[61]

The theory of organic evolution is a logical corollary of atheism. If God does not exist – as humanists teach – that leaves only one explanation for the origin of the universe and of man: the theory of organic evolution. Humanists regard the universe as self-existent and not created, and they believe man has emerged as a result of a continuous process.[62] They believe that man has developed from lower animals and has made enormous progress since his first appearance on earth. They have theorized then that man can enjoy unlimited potential.

The humanists would like to convince us that humanism means the same as being a humanitarian. Since humanists deny all absolutes, they cannot consistently talk about any obligation to do good for anyone. Joseph Fletcher, a prominent humanist bioethicist, opposes sending food and other supplies to countries, which have "exceeded their biological carrying capacity."[63] If we feed overcrowded nations, which refuse to practice birth control, we are behaving in an immoral manner in his view.

The New Eugenics and Humanism Go Together

The word "eugenics" derives from a Greek term meaning, "well born." Supposedly, it is the science, which attempts to improve the human race through the control of heredity factors. The philosophy of eugenics is the idea that the best of the human species ought to be preserved – and the inferior eliminated.

The father of modern eugenics was Francis Galton (1822-1911). Galton believed that, because exceptional types of animals can be developed by selective breeding (along with the elimination of inferior offspring), the same principle could and should be applied to humans. Galton, a cousin of Charles Darwin, was significantly influenced by Darwin's book, "The Origin of Species" (1859).

It is evident that Galton's ideas (and those expressed by Darwin) and the political philosophy eventually adopted by Adolph Hitler are very similar. The Nazi philosophy says that the weak and flawed people of our society should be eliminated and is being promoted by many leaders in governmental and educational circles today. In 1972, Dr. William Gaylin, a professor of psychiatry and law at Columbia University, made a speech in which he stated, "… It used to be easy to know what we wanted for our children, and now the best for our children might mean deciding which ones to kill… "[64]

Many leaders of scientific and political influence in our society are in agreement with Dr. Gaylin. Humanism has promoted abortion, genetic engineering, and human cloning, along with the new eugenics. Human cloning is anther step in man's thinking which continues the "slippery slope" process of believing that humans are just animals to be experimented on or eliminated if need be.

Cloning a single animal, the sheep "Dolly" (in Scotland, 1997) involved the deaths of 277 developing embryos and resulted in some duplicate lambs being born with severe and lethal birth defects. Who cares if, because of the differences in the way sheep and human cells divide, cloning humans poses greater difficulty resulting in even more deaths and lethal birth defects? We are all just "animals" anyway (Romans 1:18-32).

We have created an atmosphere in this country that says life is not sacred. It is cheap, especially if you can develop it in a test tube or petri dish. We are also saying that we don't need God anymore, we are gods. Richard Seed, the Chicago scientist on the verge of human cloning, says, "Cloning and the programming of DNA is the first serious step in becoming one with God."

This philosophy, which has developed in the last generation, has sown death and reaped a whirlwind of pain. The apostle Paul said, "Do not be deceived, God is not mocked; for whatever a man sows, this he will also reap" (Galatians 6:7).

The harvest on our horizon is EUTHANASIA. Former Surgeon General, Dr. C. Everett Koop says that euthanasia will dwarf abortion in its practice. Ironically, the generation that has forced death upon this culture will likely die at the hands of their children, or at least the children that made it into this world alive.

The Skilled Helper's Response

The Bible is filled with teaching from God that confirms the "sanctity of life" (Genesis 9:4-6)! Not only the sanctity of life but the HOPE of life after DEATH! In fact, the ultimate promise of God is that there is a quality of life after death, which transcends anything experienced here on this earth (II Peter 3:11-13; Revelation 21:1-4).

What could possibly make life more meaningless for man than to know that his trials, troubles, and struggles with temptations will be rewarded with nothingness? Only the God of the Bible can give us the hope of experiencing the bliss of ETERNITY with Him (Philippians 3:7-11).

The Skilled Helper must counsel against unethical and immoral practices. He/she must continue to confirm the sanctity of life and the practice of holy living before God, so that the counselee will experience the true fullness of life (John 10:10).

Review Questions

1. What does the Bible say about abortion?
2. What are some of the psychological effects of an abortion?
3. Why is pornography harmful?
4. What are the dangers of "materialism?"
5. Why do Humanism and Atheism go together?
6. How would you define "euthanasia?"
7. What is the significance of "cloning?"
8. Who is Joseph Fletcher?

Chapter Twelve

THE WORK OF THE HOLY SPIRIT

We live under the dispensation of the Holy Spirit of God. It is the fulfillment of the promise of Jesus (John 14:16, 17; 16:13). The Holy Spirit converts sinners (through the Word of God), dwells in the Christian, comforted the apostles and abides even today as the Comforter (I Corinthians 6:19).

God designed that the Holy Spirit be manifested in three ways:

1. The Baptism of the Holy Spirit (Acts 1:5-8; 2:1-5).
2. The Indwelling of the Holy Spirit (Acts 2:38; 5:32).
3. The Miraculous Gifts of the Holy Spirit (Acts 8:15-18; I Corinthians 12:12-31).

Jesus said that those who came to be continual believers in Him would receive the Spirit of God to indwell their bodies, but only after He had been glorified (John 7:37-39). The indwelling of the Holy Spirit did not guarantee that the baptized believer would have miraculous powers. God had purposed miracles for the early church (Hebrews 2:3, 4).

The Holy Spirit is a Divine Entity

The New Testament brings together the divinity and names them as composing the Godhead. Jesus, after his resurrection and just before his ascension, gave his commission to his apostles, and said, "Therefore go and make disciples of all the nations, baptizing them into the name of the Father and of the Son and of the Holy Spirit" (Matthew 28:19). Here we have the simple act of baptism as commanded to be done in the name of the Godhead. This brings one into a covenant relationship with the Father and the Son, and the Holy Spirit (Romans 8:16, 17). The Holy Spirit is associated here with the Father and the Son; the Holy Spirit is thus connected with the salvation of man.

The Doctrine of The Godhead

The doctrine of the Godhead is revealed only in the Bible; no one can learn of Christ the Savior or the Holy Spirit from nature. It is important that we have correct views concerning the Bible teaching on the Godhead. If we entertain false conceptions and wrong views of the Godhead, we will not be able to understand the nature of the Holy Spirit, our system of faith, and how He helps us as counselors. Some have taught that the Godhead is a threefold manifestation of one person. This theory makes the Godhead one God.

There is a sense in which the three are one, but this unity does not destroy the three distinct personalities of the Godhead. Another false view is that there are three Gods; this theory ignores the unity of the Godhead. Both of the above views contradict the teachings of the Bible that God is three persons, yet one in essence and purpose.

Jesus constantly referred to God as his Father and as a distinct person from himself (John 17:1-5). Jesus also promised to send the Comforter from the Father (John 15:26). Jesus could not send the Holy Spirit as a third divine person if the Godhead were only one person showing himself in three different ways (Acts 1:6-8).

The Godhead evidently was revealed to men in the Bible as three persons, and not as three representations of one person. All the members of the Godhead are of the same nature; hence, they partake of the nature of the other members of the Godhead (Genesis 1:26).

The Holy Spirit is a Person

The works of the Holy Spirit manifest His personality. He speaks, witnesses, teaches, guides, leads, and forbids (I Timothy 4:1; John 15:26; 14:26; 16:13; Acts 16:6-10). He directs the apostles and the church. He speaks to us through His Word.

The apostle Paul was forbidden (by the Holy Spirit) to speak in Asia. He wanted to go into Bithynia but the Spirit would not permit it. He passed on to Troas, where in a vision by night he received a call to come into Macedonia. The Spirit had thus forbidden him to preach in Asia and Bithynia and had led him to preach in Macedonia.

The characteristics of the Holy Spirit declare His personality. He possesses a "mind" (Romans 8:27). He has "knowledge" (I Corinthians 2:11).

He has "affections" and the highest of all affections is attributed to the Spirit (Romans 15:30). He possesses a "will" (I Corinthians 12:11).

The slights and injuries suffered by the Holy Spirit declare his personality. He can be "grieved" (Ephesians 4:30). He can be "resisted" (Acts 7:51). He can be "blasphemed" (Matthew 12:32).

The Holy Spirit does the work of deity. He helped "create" the universe (Psalm 104:30). He "regenerates" man (John 3:3-8). He "strengthens" the believer (Ephesians 3:16). He will "resurrect" the body (Romans 8:11). He "performs" miracles (miraculous gifts of the Spirit, I Corinthians 12:4-11).

The work of the Holy Spirit is implied in the very definition of the Greek word, PNEUMA, which can be translated, "wind," "breath" or "spirit" (John 3:8; II Thessalonians 2:8). The Holy Spirit is deity, is a person, and is a part of and works with the eternal Godhead. The Spirit wants to work in our lives (Ephesians 5:18).

The Holy Spirit wants to help us as counselors by encouraging, teaching, strengthening, empowering, and giving us wisdom to help others deal with their stresses and distresses in life (Ephesians 3:16; Philippians 2:13; James 1:5-8).

The Gift of The Holy Spirit

In agreement with Acts 2:38 and 5:32, the apostle Paul says that God had given the Galatian Christians the Spirit as they heard the word of faith, obeyed it and became His sons (Galatians 3:2, 5, 26-29; 4:6; I Thessalonians 4:8). Jesus said the apostles' relationship to the Spirit of God was going to change – something new was going to occur. In working with the apostles, Jesus sent them out on what is called the "limited commission," and gave them the power to perform miracles (Matt. 10:5-8). The Spirit had been "with" them, in the sense of working side by side with them. The Spirit undoubtedly was with them when Jesus sent them out on the limited commission and they performed miracles. But the Spirit will now be "in" them in an indwelling sense (John 14:17).

A. T. Robertson reveals that the Greek in John 14:17 refers to the Spirit as having been "by your side," but will be "in you, in your hearts."[65] So twice in the book of John, Jesus promises that all believers and the apostles would receive the Holy Spirit as an abiding, indwelling presence (John 7:38, 39; 14:16-18).

It is in the letters of Paul, particularly, that we learn not only the fact of the indwelling, but also the function of the indwelling Spirit of God. The Spirit is a SEAL of God unto salvation. Sealing the Christian is a work of God through the Spirit (Ephesians 1:13, 14). The Father is the Sealer and the Spirit is the Seal. The word SEAL means, "to set a mark upon something by the impress of a seal, to stamp, to confirm, and authenticate." (Thayer) Thus, God has approved us as being His by giving us His Spirit (Romans 8:15-17; I John 3:23, 24; 4:13).

We know that we have the Spirit as our seal because we have God's word on it, and therefore by knowledge of that word and faith in Christ, we believe it as surely as we believe we have forgiveness of sins when we repent and are baptized in the name of Christ (Acts 2:38).

If a demon (spirit) can enter the body of a human being, then the idea of God's Spirit indwelling the Christian is an established fact (Matthew 12:43-45; Acts 19:11-20). "Demon possession" is not the same as demon influence (Ephesians 6:10-12; I Peter 5:8; II Corinthians 11:3, 14, 15).

Demon possession ended in the first century along with the phasing out of miraculous gifts (I Corinthians 13:8-13). The Holy Spirit is our motivation to Godly living. The apostle Paul says that the work of the Spirit is to motivate the Christian to do and be good (Ephesians 4:29-30; Philippians 2:13). The knowledge of the Spirit's indwelling gives us the power to enable us as Christians to overcome the lusts of the flesh (I Corinthians 6:19, 20).

The Intercession of The Holy Spirit

It is evident from Scripture that the Holy Spirit is deeply interested in the prayers and affairs of men (Romans 8:26, 27). He is concerned about our burdens and helps to bear them. Aware of the weaknesses of the saints, the Spirit expresses their needs and pleads their cause before the Father. The word "intercession" has its origin in the Greek word "entunchano" and it means to, "primarily to fall in with, meet with in order to converse."[66] Thus, the indwelling of the Spirit is a fact and the comforting work He does strengthens the Christian to face all temptations (I Corinthians 10:13).

Church members may live on two levels: The LOWER level, the carnal level, which consists of the works of the flesh (I Corinthians 3:1-4), and the HIGHER level, which consists of the fruit of the Spirit (Romans 8:5-14).

The Christian who enjoys the Christian life and develops most nearly into the likeness of Christ must live upon the higher plane. Those who live upon the lower plane live as the world does. They are those who live after the flesh or the world (Hebrews 5:11-14).

The higher, spiritual level is where the fruit of the Spirit is seen. The lower level of life is the fleshly, the carnal level, the level of the world; the higher level of life is the spiritual, the Christian level (James 3:17, 18). There are just two ways of living: "in the flesh" and "in the Spirit."

The CARNAL nature and the SPIRITUAL nature are sometimes both in the same person. There is a conflict between the two – which shall prevail (Romans 7:14-24)? To bear fruit is the supreme and ultimate purpose of the Christian life (John 15:1-11). The test of the Christian life is "the fruit of the Spirit" (I Thessalonians 5:19). Therefore, we must strive to be "filled with the Spirit" (Ephesians 5:18).

The Works of The Flesh

The word "flesh" in the Greek is SARX, which means, "carnal, fleshly, sinful, worldly, or in reference to nature" (Galatians 5:19-21). Those who are living on the lower plane of the flesh are minding the things of the flesh (Romans 8:5-14). They do the things of the flesh (James 3:13-16).

Works of the flesh may mean the frailty of human nature and its corruption by sin (Romans 6:11-18). These works make a very black list and include, "sensuality" and "uncleanness" in their most enticing and debasing forms.

"Idolatry" is also mentioned and it sums up all evil and arises from putting anything and everything before or in place of God. "Selfishness" is also listed, and is the root which produces "fornication" (sexual immorality), "witchcraft," "hatred," "discord," "jealousy," "fits of anger," "factions," "divisions," "envy," "orgies," "drunkenness," and such like (Romans 1:18-32).

"Self-indulgence" is the attitude that fires the passions that lead to "the works of the flesh" (James 4:1-6). These "works of the flesh" are very similar to "the works of the devil" (I John 3:8). The "mind of the flesh" is enmity against God (Romans 8:7). The "mind of the flesh" is death (Romans 8:6). This is why those who do the "works of the flesh" cannot please God (Romans 8:8).

The Fruit of The Spirit

The Holy Spirit operates through the Word; dwells in Christians; and Christian conduct is the "fruit of the Spirit" (Galatians 5:22-26) One might call this fruit the gift of the Spirit, for without the Spirit it would not be possible for us to consistently have or produce this kind of fruit (II Peter 1:4-11). The chief work that the Holy Spirit has with Christians is to develop them into the likeness of Christ. One of the primary objectives of the Holy Spirit dwelling in Christians is to reproduce in them the glory of the personality of Christ (Philippians 2:5, 13).

The glory of Christianity is the fruit of the Holy Spirit (Galatians 5:24). It should be observed that spiritual growth and development of Christians conform to the laws of the Holy Spirit's working. No one can bear the fruit of the Spirit who does not have the indwelling Spirit in him, and in order to allow the Spirit to work in us, we must crucify the passions of the flesh that enslave us.

There are nine different kinds of fruit mentioned in the Bible (Galatians 5:22, 23). Those mentioned are: "Love," "joy," "peace," "patience," "kindness," "goodness," "faithfulness," "meekness," "self-control," and against such there is no law. As Christians trust in God and live faithful to His word, the fruit of the Spirit is revealed as the natural result.

The Leading of The Holy Spirit

A distinction should be drawn between the miraculous and extraordinary manifestations of the Holy Spirit and the common or ordinary manifestations. The Holy Spirit in some extraordinary way led Jesus. In like manner the Holy Spirit led the apostles (Acts 2:1-8). The Holy Spirit also leads Christians through the Word and by influence. We must submit to the influence of the Spirit (Ephesians 5:18).

In the New Testament the disciples were given the Great Commission (Matthew 28:19, 20). The baptized believers were taught to make disciples and baptize them as they went about preaching the Word of God. The baptized believers were taught how to live the Christian life. The guidance of the Holy Spirit is as important in the Christian life as it is in leading unbelievers to Christ. But all of this is done through the guidance of the Word of God (Romans 10:14-17). The teaching of the Holy Spirit is through the Word. It cannot be emphasized too often that the Holy Spirit in all of His work uses the instrumentality of truth (John 16:13-15). The Holy Spirit speaks through the word of God (I Timothy 4:1, 2).

The Holy Spirit uses truth in conversion today (through the written Word) as distinct from using error (Acts 16:14). The Holy Spirit gave all truth to the apostles and the church was to follow the doctrines and practices established by them (Acts 2:42). The truth was established by the Holy Spirit through examples, commands, and applied inferences that were given to the early church (I Corinthians 11:2).

There is not a shadow of evidence in the Bible that a human heart was ever changed from sin to holiness by the force of error (James 5:16). No man was ever moved to follow truth by believing lies. No soul ever thrived upon believing lies (John 8:32). A sincere and honest acceptance of faults is not enough to please God; he/she must also have the desire to obey the truth (II Thessalonians 2:8-12).

In some way that only God knows, the Holy Spirit does guide us. God works in us and the Holy Spirit is His agent (I John 3:23, 24). God will give us wisdom undoubtedly through His Spirit (James 1:5-8). God strengthens us through His Spirit (Ephesians 3:16). We can be filled with His Spirit (Ephesians 5:18). We have the indwelling of His Spirit (Acts 5:32). We can grieve His Spirit (Ephesians 4:30). We can quench His Spirit (I Thessalonians 5:19).

There is a difference between the Holy Spirit "guiding" and "inspiring" man! When guided by the Holy Spirit, He influences us to do the will of God. When the early disciples were given the miraculous gifts and inspired by the Holy Spirit, they were directed by Him to speak and do God's will (John 14:15-17; 25, 26).

The Anointing of The Holy Spirit

It is the indwelling of the Holy Spirit that is described as the "anointing" of the Holy Spirit (I John 2:20-27). In this text, the apostle John was dealing with false teaching about the true nature of Christ. He was encouraging the church to follow the teaching they had already received about the nature of Christ and to allow the Holy Spirit (the anointing) to work in them, convicting them of the truth (Philippians 2:13).

To be guided or led by the New Testament is to be led by the Holy Spirit (I Timothy 4:1-5). The Holy Spirit leads everyone the same way and what the New Testament says it says to everyone alike, other than some statements directed only to the apostles (I Corinthians 4:6). Therefore, if the Holy Spirit is leading us, then the written Word of God is leading us! The Holy Spirit speaks to us and leads through and in conjunction with the Word of God. The Holy Spirit led the apostles into all truth about the church and the traditions that should be followed by all Christians (Ephesians 2:19-22).

The Power of Prayer in Counseling

To the Christian, praying should be an automatic way of life especially if he/she is a counselor. If we are Christian counselors, then we are true believers in the truth and power of God's Word and His promises. He does promise to be with us and to answer our prayers, as long as they are within His will (I John 5:14, 15). We must ask in faith, knowing and believing that God will give us the wisdom we need to help others and to be a Christian example to them (James 1:5-8).

Prayer accomplishes several things. It releases the person to God and it reminds us that we are not the one who is the final resource in this life, and that we are not in charge. We need the direct "intervention" of God in the life of the person to guide, sustain, and comfort him. I have discovered that by keeping a list and praying for my counselees' specific concerns and issues, when he walks into my office, I know what his concerns are because I have been reminded through prayer the previous week.

The importance of the power of God working in our lives and in the counselees' life cannot be overestimated. Some counselors reserve a few minutes between sessions in order to pray for the next person they will be seeing for counseling. Others have set aside a small office nearby just for prayer and meditation for the counselee. Another way of praying is for the counselor to look over the schedule of those whom he or she will be seeing on that day and to set aside a few minutes of quiet time in the office. The counselor should visualize each person walking into the office and sitting down. Pray specifically for the person's needs, for a listening ear and sensitivity toward the person, and for the wisdom of the Holy Spirit to guide your counseling efforts.

The core of counseling is prayer. But too little is said about prayer in counseling and too little is written about its use during the session and between sessions. This is not a chapter on how to pray or what posture you should have for prayer or what should be said in prayer. The Bible emphasizes that sincerity, intensity, humility, and thankfulness in a believer's heart, are the most important ingredients in a prayer (Luke 18:1-14; Colossians 4:2).

God does not want "canned" or "repetitive" prayers, instead He wants us to speak from the heart in simple terms what we feel and need of Him (Matthew 6:5-8). We can have confidence that with the Holy Spirit's help (Romans 8:26, 27) and the sympathy of Jesus Christ as our High Priest in prayer (Hebrews 2:16-18; 4:15, 16), we can be effective, as counselors and skilled helpers, striving to give others hope and purpose in their lives (James 5:16).

Prayer is not something to just tack on at the end of a counseling session to make it seem like it is truly "Christian Counseling." Prayer reflects a dependency upon the Lord that brings us to the point of knowing where our power is and humbly submitting to Him.

We as counselors can be more effective if we remind ourselves at the beginning of each day and each session that God is the one who will effect change and healing within the session. Such an attitude can and will make a difference in our success as counselors.

The Power of Prayer and Agape Love

Early on in my ministry an older woman in our congregation entered my office with a complete disdain for her husband. She told me that she didn't love him anymore and wanted to live alone the rest of her life. I didn't know this couple too well, other than they were old (actually in their mid-sixties) and seemed to get along during church services and when I visited them in their home. The more I talked to her I was able to find out that they hadn't gotten along for a long time, and she felt she didn't love him anymore and wanted to get out of the marriage. She wanted to be free! As a young minister, who was not old enough to have the insight into such problems, I didn't know what to say to a woman in her sixties, who had been married for forty years.

I listened to her for over an hour and finally I asked her to come back next week for another session and we would discuss it further. I didn't know what else to do or say at the time. It was evident that she felt estranged from her husband and didn't think he cared about her or treated her right. She didn't think that there was any hope for their marriage to last because she didn't love him anymore. What do you say to such a woman, when you are just a young minister half her age with half her experience and knowledge about life?

It is in times like these that you begin to again appreciate the privilege and promise of God to hear your prayers. The apostle Paul said, "Do not be anxious about anything, but in everything, by prayer and petition, with thanksgiving, present your requests to God. And the peace of God, which transcends all understanding, will guard your hearts and your minds in Christ Jesus" (Philippians 4:6, 7).

I was certainly "anxious" and needed some answers quickly. I prayed almost everyday during the week before my next appointment with this lady (Mary). All I could think of was; "how am I going to get Mary to love her husband (Joe) again." Finally, the session began and I could think of nothing in particular to say to Mary as she again stated she didn't love Joe anymore. I then began to discuss the concept of love and how God told us to (agape) love others.

The Greek word AGAPE is the noun form of the word for "unconditional" love; it is a love that requires of us that we do what is best for another person. I explained to Mary that "agape" love is unconditional and does not require an emotional attachment and therefore can be commanded by God (Matthew 7:12).

I finally asked Mary if she could still love Joe with the kind of love that Jesus said we should have for our neighbor (Matthew 19:19)? She thought about it for a moment and said, "I don't think I could, because he doesn't show me any love or attention and I have put up with him for forty years." I then asked her if she could love her enemies like Jesus commanded us to do (Matthew 5:43-48) and if so, could she love her husband as an enemy? She had to think about that for a long time, and then she said, "maybe I could love him as an enemy but I still want a divorce."

Finally, I asked Mary to try loving Joe as an enemy for one month, praying for God to help her, and then come back and let me know how things were developing. She reluctantly said she would do at least that much, but she said, "I don't want to love him at all and I think this is a waste of time."

One of the things I learned from this counseling experience is that God really does answer prayer when you don't know what to do, and you pray in faith. I surprised myself when I came up with that strategy for Mary, because I hadn't thought of it until that moment.

Another thing I learned, as a "rookie" counselor, is that people don't come to your counseling office, when they have given up "all" hope. If they didn't have some hope that you, as a counselor, could help them, they wouldn't bother to ask for it.

Mary had told me there wasn't any hope for their marriage, but in reality, she was hoping that I might have something to say to give her hope. She came into my office approximately six weeks after the last counseling session, when I had given her the advice to love her husband like an enemy. She was very excited and said, "You know, I can't believe it, I started trying to please him, and I stopped nagging him, because I tried to love him like an enemy and do what's best for him." "You'll never guess what happened a few days later." "He has been so good to me and we have gone out to dinner together and are much closer now than we have ever been." "Do you suppose that this is an answer to my prayers, when in the past I have been so angry that God didn't hear me?" She went on to say that she didn't think she would need my counseling services any longer.

I wish I could take credit for the success of this counseling story, but I can't. I believe that the power of prayer solved this problem. I believe now that there is not a permanent solution to our problems without intense prayer and a willingness to do the will of God. Thank you Holy Spirit and thank you Jesus and thank you God for being there to help me save a marriage and possibly the souls of two wonderful Christians. I couldn't have done it without you.

May God bless faithful counselors, who know where the truth and power is, and never stop putting their faith in God and never stop caring for people.

Review Questions

1. How do we know the Holy Spirit is a person?
2. What does the Holy Spirit do for us as Skilled Helpers?
3. What is the intercession of the Holy Spirit?
4. How does the Holy Spirit lead us?
5. How should the Skilled Helper use prayer when counseling others?
6. What was Mary's problem with her husband?
7. Why is prayer the core of counseling?
8. How would you describe the "Godhead?"

Chapter Thirteen

THE TRUTH ABOUT SUFFERING

The topic of this chapter is pain. If you are like me, you want to avoid it. But what do you do when it comes anyway? How do you explain the deaths that visit us despite our best efforts to avoid them? How do you explain the deaths of innocent children or adults, when it seems they did not deserve to die an untimely or horrible death? How do you explain the tragedy of a child suffering with pain from cancer?

This is where I believe that humanistic psychology fails in its explanation and Christianity supports us, for in psychology suffering has no meaning, while in Christianity it has great meaning (I Peter 4:12-19). To the humanistic psychologist, suffering is unfortunate and a tragedy that has no meaning. The psychologist may say, "It's too bad you had such a misfortune, but once you become fully aware and self-actualized, you'll find that type of thing won't happen anymore." He may say, "Let's see if we can't organize your life to avoid those kinds of mistakes."

Christianity, on the other hand, says that suffering can be redemptive. Not all suffering, but any suffering that is joined to Christ's. That doesn't mean the church requires you to formally make a declaration of intent whenever you're in pain. It seems to be a fact that there is a positive growth factor in suffering, especially if it is for the cause of Christ (James 1:2-4; I Peter 3:14).

Suffering and The Christian Faith

When considering the problem of suffering, it is quite obvious that most of our suffering is a consequence of sin. There is a vast amount of suffering in the world as a natural consequence of the sins of those who have gone on before us. It is evident that history is full of examples of nations suffering because of their sins (Psalm 9:17-20).

Men of the world cannot relate to a God who allows suffering. They assume then, that the idea of a loving and all-powerful God is not credible. The problem of suffering and pain has continued to challenge thinking men of faith. It would be presumptuous of me to assume that I, or any man of faith, can explain all aspects of pain and suffering.

It is realized by believers that the secret things of God belong to Him (Deuteronomy 29:29). God did not intend for us to understand all things or be able to explain all things. He does expect us to live by faith in the unseen works of the Lord, and believe in His love and promises for us (Hebrews 11:1, 6).

Men ask the question, "How can a so-called loving and all-powerful God allow the innocent to suffer?" It seems inconsistent with a God, who supposedly forgives and blesses His children. How can He allow people to starve to death through no fault of their own? As a counselor, I don't have the answers to all of the questions that are asked in regards to God's power and willingness to save or not save innocent people from pain and suffering. I do believe that we, as Christians, need to find a biblical principle to give to the people we are trying to teach that is a logical and reasonable explanation for the suffering of innocent people.

God Created Man as a Free Moral Agent

There is one point that is worth examining, and that is, God created man as a free, moral agent. He is allowed to make his own decisions without God overpowering him or orchestrating his decisions. God gave human beings the capacity to make decisions, which means that He wants man to make his own decisions (I John 5:3).

Thus, this power of choice, together with the fact that the material universe is governed by natural laws, must inevitably result in a certain amount of suffering. If man, by his free will, is to glorify God, and this is the purpose for which he was created (Isaiah 43:7), he must be free to make mistakes, which will inevitably bring about the consequences of pain and suffering.

The question must be asked, "What sort of world would this be if God were to intervene with a miracle every time an innocent person faced suffering, thereby suspending natural law?" It would seem logical that "natural law," which we depend on so frequently and faithfully each day of our lives, would be so random, haphazard and undependable that human existence, as we know it, would be impossible.

Not only would a consistent, dependable law be unavailable to us, our free will would be diminished. Wouldn't we be no more than puppets on a string, bobbing to and fro as the Lord saved us from one crisis to another?

Would we really have the choice to make a bad decision and suffer the consequences?

The very fact that there are consequences for bad choices creates opportunities for us to grow in knowledge and faith. It allows us to make better choices and develop patience and a proper perspective about life. It allows us to be properly nurtured and admonished in the Lord, which in turn helps us to produce spiritual fruit in our life (Hebrews 12:6-13).

What Are Other Benefits From Suffering?

The existence of pain in the animal world allows for animals to protect themselves. Pain serves as a contributor to animal preservation even as it does for humans. Pain is a phenomenon of the brain. Since the brains of animals are less sophisticated emotionally than humans, it need not be assumed that they are as intensely affected by pain. A crab for instance, will continue to eat and apparently relish a smaller crab, while being itself slowly devoured by a larger one. This shows that a crab can feel scarcely any pain, since the almost universal effect of pain is to destroy the pleasure of eating.

Suffering also contributes to the spiritual betterment of man. Suffering connected with sudden natural disasters enforces the realization that one's life on earth is both certain and uncertain. It reinforces the fact that man should lead a righteous life and be willing to give serious thought to man's questions about God and the proper response to Him.

Suffering also brings about a since of "community" and avails man of the opportunity and the privilege to help his fellow man in crisis. Such suffering brings out the best in man towards his neighbor. It triggers a loving response towards others, and in the church it reminds us of the brotherhood of the body of Christ. Such crises serve as a reminder to the believer that this world is temporal and not his home (Philippians 3:20, 21). The terrible tragedy of the attacks (by terrorists) on the World Trade Center, Pentagon and the plane crash in Pennsylvania on September 11, 2001, has revealed such a response.

Indeed, suffering in general keeps us from falling too deeply in love with this world, and thereby we are encouraged to desire a permanent abode in heaven. Suffering reveals the limitations of frail man and thus encourages us to plumb the depths of prayer and develop a deep, abiding relationship with and appreciation for our Lord (Philippians 4:6, 7).

Christianity vs. Humanism

Christianity is often contrasted unfavorably to humanism because humanists supposedly care more about people. You will hear it said that the humanist is more concerned with justice and the relief of suffering than the Christian, who it is argued, has given up on the world. This argument, of course, ignores the massive fact of practical Christian charity in the world – the schools, orphanages, hospitals and relief agencies. But it does not even hold up on a theoretical basis.

It should be plain from the argument of the previous part of this chapter that the Christian attitude toward suffering is a good deal more humanistic than the humanist one. The humanist viewpoint is, in reality, the one that has given up on the world for it has absolutely nothing to say about the misery of man and provides no hope for his future.

All that a strict humanist has to say to most of the human race living or dead is, "I'm sorry, but that is how the ball bounces." The Christian attitude, on the other hand, is not willing to come to terms with a scheme in which most of human travail means nothing and comes to nothing. Rather, Christians believe that God preserves every soul, who would seek to be righteous and Christ-like (John 5:28, 29).

Is Suffering Avoidable?

Christianity maintains that suffering is a necessary part of redemption. Because it is necessary for us, it follows that no matter how people organize their lives they will not be able to avoid it. And this seems to me a fairly accurate description of our experience. The Bible tells us that all people, both Christian and non-Christian, will suffer at times in their lives (Matthew 5:45).

Humanistic psychology has a different account of things. Suffering, it says, is a foolish mistake and moreover, an avoidable one. Whether you go to a humanistic psychologist or a behaviorist or one who practices Rational-Emotive Therapy, there will be this very strong suggestion that you can get control of your life and overcome all of your problems. Of course, to some extent, you can overcome many of your problems. But to believe that we have total control of our destiny and life is the height of arrogance. We must, as Christians, acknowledge that only God has complete control of our destiny. We must show unbelievers that God really does care for them (I Peter 5:7).

Helping Those Who Are Suffering

To the Christian, who wants to help others, the idea of explaining and analyzing pain and suffering may be a logical exercise (Philippians 4:11-13). But to the person being helped that has a limited or no Bible knowledge, and no real relationship with God, the idea that suffering (especially the suffering of innocent people) can be a positive experience for growth and contentment, is a foreign concept.

We, as Christians, must be patient and allow people to grow into an understanding of how pain and suffering are a necessary part of life. We must be ready to give an answer to those who ask us about the hope that is in us (I Peter 3:15). We must teach the Bible to them and help them to understand that a crisis is not all bad and that suffering, whether innocently or not, can be productive in a person's life, if he/she will learn to trust in the Lord (Romans 8:28).

This is a mighty task, but one that encompasses the whole of the work of a Christian who wants to help people who are hurting. It is the work of a Skilled Helper to help create in the unbeliever an every-abiding faith in God to help him/her solve his/her problems.

Review Questions

1. Do you believe that suffering is avoidable? Why?
2. How does pain and suffering discipline us?
3. What does Romans 8:28 mean to you?
4. Why did God create man as a free moral agent?
5. How has suffering and pain made you stronger in your life?
6. How should a Christian describe the purpose of suffering to a non-Christian?
7. How does Humanism, as a theory, describe suffering?
8. Why do Christian organizations create more relief agencies than do others?

Chapter Fourteen

CREATED IN GOD'S IMAGE

This chapter will discuss the philosophy behind Temperament Therapy. This theory is basic to the belief we are created by God with different temperaments (Genesis 1:26). The "temperament" in simple terms, is the genetic, inborn part of man that determines how we react to people, places and things. There are certain characteristics and traits that are a part of us, and Temperament Therapy reveals what they are. These traits reveal how we interpret our environment and interact with it.

Temperament Therapy is a brand new therapeutic discipline. Heretofore, the Christian community has simply taken the therapeutic methods developed by the secular community such as Reality Therapy by Glasser or Client-Centered Therapy by Carl Rogers or Psychoanalysis by Freud or Behavioral Therapy by Skinner and applied them with a biblical approach. But all these therapies are based on one assumption – that man evolved and that he is his own god, and therefore, has within himself the solutions to his problems. Remember that the "temperament" is "who you are" (how God made you) and the "personality" is "who you portray yourself to be" (how you act in accordance with your interpretation of your environment).

Temperament Therapy, a biblical approach to behavioral change, is a very new and exciting therapeutic discipline. This therapy was developed (through the National Christian Counselors Association) by people, who believe in God, and desire for it to be used for the good of others. When a counselor learns and understands the temperaments and how they work, he quickly realizes that he is learning very deep and private things about another human being. This confidential information could be very dangerous in the hands of the wrong person.

Temperament Testing

Since the Temperament is "who you are," it is advantageous to study it in terms of knowing the basic traits and characteristics of a person you are counseling. This requires a "profile" vehicle in order to determine, with some scientific credibility, the exact temperament or temperament blend a counselee may have. The Temperament Analysis Profile was created by the N.C.C.A. based on the "Firo-B," a test created by Dr. Will Schutz of the Department of Psychiatry, Albert Einstein College of Medicine, Yeshiva University. This profile was developed for the purpose of determining a person's temperament characteristics and traits.

The Temperament Analysis Profile is a test the N.C.C.A., through the years of practical application, has found to be accurate beyond question. When its findings are used in the counseling office, the results save countless hours of counseling time and will give him/her, as a counselor, a unique understanding of the counselee that was impossible before testing.

The Firo-B test results are not only important in understanding the behavior of man, but they are also invaluable, because their practical application by the counselor can affect changes that will bring the counselee to a lasting emotional well-being and spiritual maturity.

The Firo-B test results also give the counselor the ability to detect areas where the counselee is vulnerable to spiritual setbacks and emotional breakdowns. These areas, once identified, can then be acted upon to stop immediate problems and to prevent future problems before they can arise.

The Firo-B questionnaire should be answered quickly. The person being tested must answer the questions in accordance with how he really sees himself, not how he thinks he should. Whoever administers the test should verify that all questions have been answered.

The Scientific Background of Temperament Theory

The scientific community has studied temperament theory and has advanced theories regarding their studies, which are varied but similar. The information given here is not an exhaustive study of temperament history but does provide a concise overview of the fundamental information available.

Another purpose of this chapter is to show the counselor that even though the secular community has a foundation for temperament theory, they have neglected to use this information. This author takes the view that this has happened because the secular community has refused to recognize that man is created, not evolved. Temperament Theory presupposes a creationist view of life.

HIPPOCRATES (460-370 B.C.)

Any study of the temperament must go back 2,400 years to the early Greek historian, Hippocrates. The study of temperaments may go back even further, to Solomon, the writer of much of the Book of Proverbs (LaHaye). Hippocrates was the first to bring to light the theory of temperament, even though he may have been building on the thoughts of Impedocles (495-435 B.C.).

According to Hippocrates, man's behavior was governed by the color of bile within a person's body. These body fluids, which he called "humors," were divided into four classifications: blood, black bile, yellow bile, and phlegm.

GALEN (131-200 A.D.)

Galen developed the first typology of temperament, which he presented in his dissertation "De Temperamentis." Galen, as his predecessor Hippocrates, searched for physiological reasons for the differences in behavior of human beings. Galen's theories have been partially proven in psychopharmacological and endocrinological research.

MAIMONIDES (1135-1204 A.D.)

Maimonides was a rabbi, physician and philosopher, who attempted to codify the Jewish oral law in his writing of the Mishna (Torah), while also writing volumes on religion and philosophy.

According to Maimonides, "humors" (temperaments) are responsible for the differences between the speed of learning, ease of understanding, excellence of memory, and also the differences between courageous versus craven attitudes.

NICHOLAS CULPEPER (1616-1654)

The four major temperaments as described by Hippocrates remained virtually unchanged until the seventeenth century with the writings of Nicholas Culpeper. Culpeper disregarded the idea of "humors" or "fluids" to define human behavior, yet he held onto the theory of temperament to identify human behavior. He felt that people were not one temperament, but were affected by two temperaments – a "dominant" and a "recessive."

IMMANUEL KANT (1724-1804)

Kant was a German philosopher, who was regarded as a "formidable intellectual giant" of his time. Anthropology has been interpreted as "...Kant's entire philosophical system." Kant believed that the vital power of the blood, and the temperature of the blood, caused the different temperaments in humans. Kant made three "blood" divisions and gauged the degree of feelings according to the temperature of the blood. The Sanguine is light-blooded and the Melancholy is heavy-blooded. The Choleric and its opposite, the Phlegmatic, have cold blood. On the basis of this philosophical observation, a person can be of only one temperament, and if two temperaments associate with one another, they will neutralize one another. On this basis, there can be no blending; i.e., Sanguine-Choleric.

ALFRED ADLER (1879-1937)

In 1927, Adler interpreted Hippocrates' four temperaments, as the Sanguine, Choleric, Melancholic and Phlegmatic. Historically, we believe that Alfred Adler was the first to develop the functioning of the temperaments. Adler believed that the Sanguine was the healthiest type because it was not subject to severe deprivations and humiliation.

Adler also believed that Sanguines have very few feelings of inferiority and strive for superiority in a happy, friendly, manner. The Choleric was the very aggressive and tensed up temperament, always striving to be on top and willing to expend great amounts of energy to get there. The Melancholy usually felt inferior and lacked initiative in overcoming most obstacles. The Melancholy was the worrier and lacked the self-discipline to make decisions when risks were involved. The Melancholy was not anti-social, but chose not to associate. The Phlegmatic was the person, who had lost contact with life and was not impressed by or with anything in it. He was also described as depressed, slow and sluggish. In 1935, Adler developed his own typology, but he did not really believe in the idea of typology. He believed that classification was an unfruitful means of dealing with humans, and was only useful to help other people learn of temperaments.

IVAN PAVLOV (1849-1936)

Pavlov was one of the most famous of Russian psychologists. He was famous for his typology of reflex in his experiments with dogs. In addition to these experiments, Pavlov observed mental patients for years. Because of the difference in the excitatory and inhibitory responses of these patients, he divided these people into the same four types as Hippocrates – the Choleric, the Melancholy, the Sanguine and the Phlegmatic. The Choleric and Melancholy were the two extreme types. The Sanguine and the Phlegmatic were the two equalizing types.

HANS J. EYSENCK (1916-)

Hans J. Eysenck, a modern contributor to the theory of temperament, is a well-known German psychologist, who received training at the University of London. He is one of the most respected psychologists of European descent living today. In his research he sought to analyze personality differences using a psycho-statistical method. Eysenck's research has led him to believe that temperament is biologically based.

TIM LAHAYE (1926-)

Dr. LaHaye is a well-known author, educator, minister and counselor. He is the founder and president of Family Life Seminars, the American Coalition for Traditional Values and the founder and past president of Christian Heritage College. Dr. LaHaye has authored at least twenty-three books, of which at least four deal with the topic of temperament and its relationship to human behavior. Although Dr. LaHaye's books are not written in a scientific format, they are important. His writings and research confirm that there are other Christian professionals, who believe that understanding temperament is imperative in the understanding of man.

This information is brief, and spans 2,400 years and represents only a minute percentage of the historical background for the study of temperament. However, we feel it is enough to show the student that there is indeed a strong historical base for evidence of the Temperament Theory.

Temperament Needs

Every individual has temperament needs to varying degrees. These temperament needs are met by drawing from the lower soul (humanistic) or from the higher soul, most commonly referred to as the spiritual. Most inter (intra)-personal conflicts are caused by:

1. Individuals attempting to meet their temperament needs in an ungodly way.
2. Temperament needs being out of balance; i.e., all the individual's energies are spent meeting some needs while other needs are ignored.
3. Reactions to unmet temperament needs.

The Therapy of Temperament, according to the N.C.C.A., is the understanding of the inner man and applying that knowledge to bring balance in all three areas of the temperament as follows:

1. INCLUSION – the intellect (and social interaction) of man.
2. CONTROL – the will or will power (decision-making process) of man.
3. AFFECTION – the emotions (expressed or wanted affection) of man.

By bringing balance into these three areas of the temperament, the foundation is laid to balance the body, soul, and spirit of man (I Thessalonians 5:23). Most of the problems that man faces today are caused by the fact that he is filled with stress. This stress makes him feel at a loss and in turmoil, and he can neither find peace with himself, nor with others. This stress (which is created by man) is caused, because he does not understand himself, and for this reason, he cannot alleviate this pressure. It is granted that if a man would trust in God and obey His commandments, he undoubtedly would understand himself better, but many times this is not the case. That is why Temperament Therapy can be so helpful in counseling.

We do not want to use this Temperament Therapy to simply make our counselees fit the mold, which we think they should fit. We want to help them come to the place where they can accept how God made them and the wonderful uniqueness of their singular personhood. We want our counselees to accept who they are and to be the very best they can be, for the glory of God. We want them to come to the place where they can, with God's help and your help, develop their strengths and control their weaknesses.

Temperament Weaknesses and Strengths

Temperament is also made up of characteristics we call strengths, and when properly used, bring glory to God. In order for our temperament strengths to bring the greatest glory to God, we must first make up our minds to focus on the good and to overlook the bad. This is done with our intellectual energies (Inclusion need area). We must then decide to bend our will, and through that strength, meet the needs of another person. This takes an act of the will (Control need area). To love unconditionally, our emotions must reach out and give love and affection to another person, regardless of our own wants and needs (Philippians 2:1-8). This is the area of emotional expression (Affection need area).

Temperament imperfections (weaknesses) determine the downfall of man. The way a man perceives himself, his world and God, will determine how he will behave. These perceptions are based in the temperament. Therefore, on the basis of this premise, the temperament is the determining factor of what we are, but our environment and our relationship with God determine what we will become.

Temperament counselors then, must identify their counselee's temperament needs and pinpoint the ones that are currently causing him/her problems. In other words, the counselee is probably experiencing a problem because he is meeting his needs in an ungodly way. Temperament counselors must identify it and replace it with a Godly method. Unmet needs become weaknesses.

The following are brief explanations of each of the temperament types:

THE MELANCHOLY

The Melancholy is plagued, all of his life, by low self-esteem and the fear of rejection, because he does not like himself. No other temperament can focus in on their imperfections and shortcomings better than the Melancholy. Their inadequacies are usually only in their own mind and are not how others perceive them; yet, this low self-esteem causes this person to constantly search the environment for messages to confirm this low self-image.

These characteristics are not set in concrete, but do affect their interpersonal relationships, unless the Melancholy can reject these tendencies. Fear of rejection causes the Melancholy to reject others first, when he perceives that he could be rejected. They project their negative attitude of themselves onto others and subconsciously do and say things, which will force the negative response they expect.

A true Melancholy is very introverted and unsure of himself; however, on the surface he appears to be competent and in control. Melancholies also can appear to be arrogant, withdrawn, aloof and looking down their noses at you. In social settings, their behavior is very direct; they can be friendly and personable, depending on the circumstances and how comfortable they feel. They usually suffer from problems such as: depression, stress, rebellion and fear.

THE CHOLERIC

The Choleric is the most difficult of all the temperaments to understand and counsel. Few of the people who come to the counseling office are the very strong Cholerics. This type of person does not seek counseling. Whenever they undertake a course of action, it is for a definite reason and they will rarely turn back from it. Whether right or wrong, they have the will power to carry it through to the end.

The person with the Choleric temperament has the best mind for envisioning new projects, and then undertaking them. They also have a knack for choosing the people who will help get the project finished, while doing exactly what the Choleric wants. The Choleric seldom sees the pitfalls in a project, but with his extremely tough will, he will carry the project through to the end regardless of the pitfalls. Their need for accomplishment is insatiable and the things they accomplish are unending, not because their plans are better, but because they will carry these plans through to the end. They will try to succeed regardless of the merit of the plan (they usually believe that their plan is always the best plan).

When carrying through with projects, they will tolerate almost no interference and do not trust anyone else to do things as well as they do. Because of this, they have a very hard time delegating authority. Hence, Cholerics are likely to burn themselves out. The Choleric needs almost constant recognition for his accomplishments and he will get angry if he does not get that recognition. The Choleric is a controlling temperament and is attracted to people he can control.

When making decisions and taking on responsibilities, the Choleric does very well and has great leadership abilities. They make very good intuitive decisions and handle responsibilities that will make other temperaments run. Their decisions are made quickly and in an intuitive manner that leaves others in their wake. When their responsibilities are undertaken, they are done so in an efficient, well-disciplined, military fashion. No other temperament is as well organized and disciplined as the Choleric.

The Choleric relates to love and affection as he does everything else. It must be on his terms and according to his standards, regardless of the other person's feelings. It is true that Cholerics express a great deal of love and affection, but these emotions are not well developed and they have a tendency to use love and affection as a means to an end.

THE SANGUINE

Sanguines, in a group of people, are the easiest to identify; they are the ones who are the center of attention, talk the loudest, tell the funniest jokes and wear the brightest colors. They bring life and energy into a room by their very presence. Their cheerfulness and humor brightens everyone's lives. When it comes to social orientation, the Sanguine is rarely found alone, and if he must be alone, he is talking on the phone, reading a book about people, watching a TV show about people, or anything that will give him the feeling that people are around or that he is involved in other people's lives. If they have been in a situation where they were not able to be with people, Sanguines will find themselves compulsively driven to be with people again.

The Sanguine is the optimistic type of person who believes life is an exciting, fun filled experience that should be lived to the fullest. Inactivity causes them stress because the pace at which they like to live their lives is fast and furious. Most of the other temperaments get tired just watching them when they are in full swing. Needing to have money at all times is quite typical of the Sanguine. It is not the money itself that they need, but what the money represents, so they can go places and do things with other people!

The Sanguine excels at things that are communication oriented, but is not patient when it comes to doing jobs. They usually do not relate well to tasks, but love to relate to people; if they do take a task, it is done as quickly as possible, so they can be with people again. They are the least disciplined and organized of all the temperaments. When relating to people, they are outgoing, enthusiastic, warm, compassionate and seem to relate well to other people's feelings, yet they can be rude and uncaring. They will walk away from you when you are in mid-sentence because they are simply not interested in what you have to say anymore, or they will be constantly searching with their eyes to find the next person with whom they will interact.

THE PHLEGMATIC

Phlegmatics are extremely slow-paced, stubborn and can let their lives become stagnant; because it takes too much effort to let their talents show forth. The person with this type of temperament goes through life doing as little as possible, as quietly as possible, expending as little energy as possible. It is not clear whether this is because they have little energy, or if it is because they refuse to use what little energy they do have. The person with the Phlegmatic temperament can go to work, sit in a cubbyhole of a room, work with figures all day, come home from work, take a nap, get up, eat, take another nap, get up, go to bed, and still have trouble getting up in the morning.

The person with the Phlegmatic temperament is task oriented and has a great capacity for tasks, which are tedious and must be performed with accuracy. They make great data processors, bookkeepers, librarians, accountants, records technicians, or museum curators. When someone is writing important books, the Phelgmatic is the best person to do and catalog the research. Any task that requires precision and accuracy, the tedium of which would irritate other temperaments, can be handled well by the Phlegmatic.

When it comes to social interactions, the Phlegmatic is quite flexible. If he wants to interact socially, he can do so for long periods of time, even though he has no need to interact. Hence, the Phlegmatic can be either task oriented or relationship oriented, depending upon the situation. The Phlegmatic has a dry sense of humor and at times can be quite humorous without even smiling. The Phlegmatic has a sense of humor that drives the other temperaments crazy. This dry, wiry humor protects him from becoming too involved with the other temperaments. For example, the Phlegmatic temperament is the only one who can handle the Choleric, for his humor leaves the Choleric so angry he will walk away from the situation. The Choleric has no way of handling the Phlegmatic or controlling him. The Phlegmatic uses his humor to actively deal with the Choleric and to keep the Choleric from pushing him into doing something. The Phlegmatic can handle himself in almost all situations and is an extremely well rounded individual.

The Balance of Temperament Needs

The most important aspect of Temperament Therapy is to understand that these temperament types are defined in terms of basic tendencies or traits and characteristics. They can be controlled in the sense of the weaknesses they create and stereotyping should be avoided. Without the results of a profile that has a credible scientific base, it is almost impossible to identify a temperament type accurately. Temperament Therapy is not to be focused on the negative aspects of the types so much as counseling the counselee on how to meet the temperament needs in a moral and Godly way. The fulfilling life God has in store for us can be found only in our willingness to accept the temperament we were created with and to recognize the weaknesses of that temperament, and with God's help, learn to control them. The Temperament Counselor can help the counselee find out what his needs are and teach the counselee how to understand and control them.

The temperament is made up of three specific areas: Inclusion, Control and Affection. Temperament has not previously been identified as a part of the precise order or balance of man. Temperament is a missing link in this balance. The spirit (the source of the will and life of man) is the binding, balancing and blending agent, which provides order within man (James 2:26).

The temperament is able to meet its needs by drawing from the regions of either the lower self (the flesh) or the higher region of the self (the soul). This higher realm is the area conducive to the Holy Scriptures. If the body and spirit are to remain in balance, these three areas (Inclusion, Control and Affection) of the temperament must be balanced. If the body and spirit are out of balance, the physical man will break down. We must know this order, and we must help provide a means to achieve balance in this order.

In Conclusion

It is the belief of this author and counselor, that the combination of Misbelief Therapy and Temperament Therapy is a very effective methodology in helping people deal with their emotional and psychological problems, because both methodologies are biblically based. Since the Temperament is "who we are" (how God made us), Temperament Therapy becomes an effective discipline for finding out how to understand our weaknesses and deal with them. Since the personality is "who we portray ourselves to be,"

Misbelief Therapy is ideal for the problems the personality creates because the personality is based on our belief systems. This means we portray ourselves in terms of what we tell ourselves, and the lies that are programmed in our mind.

Both methodologies are very effective in helping man find balance and the perfect place that God has designed for him. These two therapies become the mechanisms by which a man/woman is given the ability to find balance of body, soul and spirit allowing him/her to be the best that God created them to be. To God be the glory!

Review Questions

1. How would you define Temperament Therapy?
2. What is meant by the concept of "temperament needs?"
3. What is the contribution that Ivan Pavlov made to Temperament Theory?
4. What is the need area called Inclusion?
5. What is the need area called Control?
6. What is the need area called Affection?
7. What contribution did Alfred Adler make to Temperament Theory?
8. How would you describe the purpose of balancing the two methodologies and their effectiveness in counseling as mentioned in this chapter?

(Footnotes)

[1] Frank Minirth, "Introduction to Psychology and Counseling," (Baker Book House, 1982) 138.
[2] William Backus & Marie Chapian, "Telling Yourself The Truth," (Bethany Publishing, 1980) 25.
[3] W. E. Vine, "Vine's Expository Dictionary of New Testament Words," MacDonald Publishing Co., 32, 33.
[4] Backus, 17.
[5] Vine, 382.
[6] Wayne Jackson, "The Bible and Mental Health," (Courier Publishers, 1998) 91.
[7] Mark P. Cosgrove, "Counseling for Anger," Word Publishing, 68.
[8] Quoted from "Making Things Right," Paul Faulkner, Sweet Publishing, 131.
[9] "Making Things Right," 132.
[10] "Dynamic Preaching," (June 1998) 15, 16.
[11] Foley, 1984.
[12] Vine, 159.
[13] Vine, 159.
[14] Bailey & Pillard, 1991.
[15] Bill Flatt, "Counseling the Homosexual," (National Christian Press, Inc., 1985) 67, 68.
[16] Paul Meier, M.D., "Christian Child-Rearing and Personality Development," Grand Rapids, Mich., Baker Book House, 55.
[17] Meier, 53.
[18] Paul Faulkner & Carl Brecheen, "What Every Family Needs," Nashville, Tenn., (Gospel Advocate Publishers, 1994) 145, 146.
[19] J. Kagen, "Psychological Review," (1958) 296-305.
[20] Ken Canfield, "The National Center For Fathering.," Manhattan, Kansas.
[21] H. Biller, "Child Development," (1969) 539-546.
[22] A. Heilbrun, "The Parent-Child Relations," (The Family Coordinator, 1976) 65-70.
[23] R. B. Berns, "Child, Family, Community," (1989) 155.
[24] B. & D. Rollins, "Contemporary Theories About The Family."
[25] James Dobson, "Focus on the Family Magazine."
[26] Smalley & Trent, "The Language of Love," 35, 36.
[27] Parad, 1965.
[28] Bard, 1974.
[29] Reprinted from JOURNAL OF PSYCHOSOMATIC RESEARCH, Vol. 11, Holmes & Rahe: "The Social Readjustment Rating Scale" pp 213-218, 1967, with permission from Elsevier Science.
[30] Elisabeth Kubler-Ross, "On Death and Dying," Copyright 1997, Simon & Schuster Publishers, adapted with permission by Scribner.
[31] Peter W. Stoner, "Science Speaks," 106, 107.
[32] Hastings, "The Inspiration of The Bible."
[33] F. F. Bruce, "New Testament Documents:Are They Reliable?" 15-17.
[34] Bruce, 16, 17.
[35] Webster's College Dictionary.
[36] International Standard Bible Encyclopedia.
[37] Charles Darwin, "The Origin of Species," London, 1859.

[38] George Wald, "Frontiers of Modern Biology in Theories of the Origin of Life," (New York, 1972) 187.
[39] Bert Thompson, "Apologetics Press."
[40] G. Parker & H. Morris, "What is Creation Science?" 16.
[41] IMPACT, "The Once and Future Universe," (1983) 705.
[42] Robert Jastrow, "Until The Sun Dies," 1977.
[43] Goldberg & Green, "Molecular Insights Into The Living Process," 1967.
[44] Thaxton, Bradley & Olsen, "The Mystery of Life's Origin," (1984) 76, 77.
[45] Thaxton, 76, 77.
[46] George Gaylord Simpson, "Tempo and Mode in Evolution."
[47] Simpson, "Tempo and Mode in Evolution."
[48] Duane Gish, "The Fossils Say No," (1979) 178.
[49] A. Morrison, "Man Does Not Stand Alone."
[50] Whitcomb & DeYoung, "The Moon and its Creation."
[51] Science Digest, 1981.
[52] Lawrence J. Crabb, Jr., "Basic Principles of Biblical Counseling," 41, 42.
[53] New World Dictionary, Second College Edition, 1974.
[54] Tim LaHaye, "Understanding the Male Temperament," Revell Co., 1975.
[55] Jay E. Adams, "Competent to Counsel," Zondervan Publishing, 1970.
[56] Backus, "Telling Yourself The Truth," (Introduction).
[57] Joseph Fletcher, "Situation Ethics."
[58] A.F.A. Journal, May 1992.
[59] Pro-Life News, July 1983.
[60] The World Dictionary.
[61] Humanist Manifestos I & II (Prometheus Books, 1973) 16.
[62] Humanist Manifestos I & II, 8.
[63] Joseph Fletcher, "Humanhood: Biomedical Ethics," (Prometheus Books, 1979) 55.
[64] Paul Marx, "Death Without Dignity," (Liturgical Press, 1975) 81.
[65] A. T. Robertson, "Word Pictures in the New Testament," Vol. 4, (Baker Book House) 253.
[66] Vine, 607.

SELECTED BIBLIOGRAPHY

Adams, Jay E.; "Competent to Counsel," Zondervan Publishing House, 1970

Adams, Jay E.; "The Christian Counselor's Manual," Zondervan Publishing House, 1973

Backus, William; Chapian, Marie; "Telling Yourself The Truth," Bethany House, 1985

Benner, David G. (editor); "Baker Encyclopedia of Psychology," Baker House, 1985

Cloud, Henry & Townsend, John; "Boundaries," Zondervan Publishing House, 1992

Crabb, Lawrence J. Jr.; "Basic Principles of Biblical Counseling," Zondervan Publishing House, 1977

Flatt, Bill W.; Flatt, Dowell; Lewis, Jack P.; "Counseling Homosexuals," Sain Publications, 1982

Gray, John; "Men Are From Mars, Women Are From Venus," Harper Publishers, 1992

Kubler-Ross, Elisabeth; "On Death and Dying," adapted with the permission of Scribner, a Division of Simon & Schuster, Copyright © 1997

Leman, Kevin & Carlson, Randy; "Unlocking The Secrets of Your Childhood Memories," Thomas Nelson Publishers, 1989

Meier, Paul D.; "Christian Child-Rearing and Personality Development," Baker Book House, 1977

Meier, Paul D.; Minirth, Frank B.; Ratcliff, Donald E.; Wichern, Frank B.; "Introduction to Psychology and Counseling," Baker Book House; Second Edition, 1991

Minirth, Frank B. & Meier, Paul D.; "Happiness Is a Choice," Baker Book House, 1978

Smalley, Gary & Trent, John; "The Language of Love," Focus on the Family, 1988

Thurman, Chris; "The Lies We Believe," Thomas Nelson Publishers, 1989

Wilson, Ken; "The Christian Home," Star Bible Publications, 2002

Wright, H. Norman; "Crisis Counseling," Regal Books, 1993